TABLE OF CONTENTS

PREFACE

We have a fascination with crime and criminals. Check your local television listings and see how many programs are dedicated to the subject. We get "real video" of police in action, investigatory reporting on crimes old and new, Judge Wapner and Judge Judy. The nation goes into gridlock over televised proceedings of O.J. Simpson, President Clinton's impeachment hearings, or Timothy McVeigh's execution; should it have been televised? Crime and criminals make the headlines in our newspapers and local TV news. We are both drawn to, and repulsed by the phenomena of crime. We discuss and dissect the reality of crime. Is there such a thing as a "hate" crime, or are all crimes "hate" crimes? Was John Hinckley, Jr. guilty of a crime for shooting President Reagan, or because of mental illness just guilty of a really bad thing? Do we blame society for producing criminals, or do we blame the individual? Should we make an attempt to rehabilitate, or is punishment the right answer? To execute, or not execute? My guess is that most of you have considered these, and many other such questions. The issues can certainly seem overwhelming, and at times some of you may even despair. But you may also at times be inclined to somehow challenge the fact of crime and criminals. It is for you that this book is written.

Some of you have always wanted to be in law enforcement. Perhaps you always wanted to be a Police Officer when you grew up. Some of you have had especially painful experiences with crime. Perhaps you or a friend or family member have been a victim. Some of you have only lately become interested in the field of criminal justice. Courses in sociology, psychology, political science, and even literature and the physical sciences can introduce you to the topic. Some of you are totally unsure of what your interests are, and are even more uncertain about your employment future. Perhaps you have heard that jobs are available in the field. A few years ago the Federal Bureau of Prisons located and built a new facility on the edge of the town where I live. Among all the issues debated locally, one of the most significant was the economic impact of a prison on the local economy. Some of my friends and family members now have "good" jobs because of the prison.

Whatever your inclination regarding criminal justice, it is most likely the case that you as yet have a limited picture of what the field is actually like, or what it has to offer. Probably cook, pilot, and dentist do not come to mind as jobs in the field. But they are. You are not probably thinking that writing and speaking are the most important tools that a law enforcement officer has in their arsenal. But again, they are. And why would a crime scene analyst with over 900 homicides investigated in his career now be taking an art class? Figure it out. The point is, you need to understand that a job, or a career in criminal justice will include so much more than most of us have ever imagined.

In this small book I try to introduce you to the idea of a career in criminal justice. I do this not through my own experience (though I did work for a while in corrections) or through the eyes of a crime and justice research institute. I do this through the eyes and lives of people who have made the kinds of decisions you are now contemplating. They have made a career in the field of criminal justice, and they are now sharing their experiences with you. Understand that the

Character Profiles are about real people. They have been right where you are now; wondering, exploring, and perhaps even planning. Though I have given them new identities to protect them personally, their lives are fully instructive to any and all who care to give pause, and examine them.

ACKNOWLEDGMENTS

Any book, even a tiny, little one like this, requires the cooperation of so many others in order to make it happen. So, here I express my gratitude to a variety of others who have had to cooperate, willingly or otherwise, to make this book a small reality. My wife Deb, and my kids, Ashlee and Billy, have had to patiently wait on me every time I said that I really had to work on the book. First, Karen Hanson, and then Jennifer Jacobson, my editors at Allyn and Bacon, often spoke needed words of encouragement, and yet deftly did the hard work of keeping me on task. Those professionals in the field of criminal justice who so freely shared with me their stories and their hopes that students would be positively impacted by them. Paige Todd, who worked so hard to put it all down on paper. To all of these, friends and colleagues, I offer my sincerest thanks

1

INTRODUCING THE IDEA OF CAREERS IN CRIMINAL JUSTICE

Step 1: Exploration and Assumptions: What to Expect About Careers

So, you are considering the career possibilities in the field of criminal justice. This can be assumed due to the fact that courses in criminal justice are not usually a part of the general education or core curriculum at most colleges. You have made a choice to take this course. Now, this does not mean that you are committed yet to the idea of a career in criminal justice. You may or may not. Some of you are certain about your future (FBI, state police, corrections, etc.) while many have only a general idea about how to get started. Others just have no idea whatsoever. You may be taking this course simply to fill your schedule, because you have friends in it, or perhaps it just sounded interesting. Whatever your case we can assume that at least for the time being, perhaps just this semester, you are at an exploratory stage regarding criminal justice. But how does one explore? Good question.

There are essentially two kinds of exploration. The first, and the one which often makes the most sense to students, is to take coursework in your area of interest. In this case, most of you are now doing this kind of exploration by taking the course for which this is a required or recommended book. I will say more about this book later. The second kind of exploration is a search, which takes you outside the "box." By this I mean, exploring disciplines, which seem to lie outside the criminal justice core. For example, ask yourself what contribution to a career in law enforcement might come from a course (or courses) of study in fields such as archeology, composition, foreign languages, business, computer science, communications, chemistry, sociology, philosophy, or history? I would suggest that there is a valid connection between criminal justice and each of these disciplines, and many others not listed. One objective of your explorations will be to discover what these contributions may be. Consider the following.

I once encountered a young man who came to me for advice on becoming a police officer. I asked

1

him what his motivation was for such a career choice. He answered, "I'm good with guns." As I pursued this line of questioning he revealed that certain cultural icons, movies, and television most prominently, had significantly impacted his perception of police work. Well, it's true that police officers must know how to use weapons. But it's also true that police officers must know how to write reports, how to make valid observations of people and situations, how to do emergency management, CPR and how to break the sad news of death to family members. The question here is, whether your explorations are sufficiently inclusive of the total package of police "work?"

Let me illustrate this further with a telling example from the field of high tech. A classmate of mine from college days earned a Ph.D. in math and went to work at one of this nation's premier research and development laboratories. His work there put him in the vanguard of fiber-optic communications technologies. After about 10 years on the job Jeff was invited back to his alma mater to meet with students and faculty and present colloquia on the latest developments in his field. Being a good friend I attended Jeff's presentations, and I was quite impressed with all he had accomplished. During the question and answer periods Jeff handled himself quite well and those in attendance seemed rightfully proud to call him one of their own. As a sociologist with special interest in career development and organizational behavior, I had an interest in some additional aspects of his work. When the time seemed right I asked, "Jeff, how much math do you do in a day?" In spite of stares from the "technophiles" in the audience I persisted in getting an answer. Jeff's response was, "Well actually, I don't do much math. For periods of time I may not do any at all. You see, I've been in management for some time now, and it's really my job to facilitate team building among others who are actually making calculations." A few years later Jeff again returned to campus, this time for a less formal visit. We talked again and I asked him about his current job responsibilities. He told me, "I've been transferred to the Netherlands. The biggest challenge is cross-cultural communication. And, it's not just language. It's the different perspectives we have." So, what should we make of this example? Well, the prime of Jeff's career is spent in work, which is not narrowly defined by his degree. In fact you can't get much more differentiated than a Ph.D. in math and a primary need for cultural sensitivity. You should understand that any career, including one in law enforcement, would likely include much the same breadth.

Consider the following. The Federal Bureau of Prisons has over 200 job categories! We are talking about guards, caseworkers, psychologists, social workers, cooks, teachers, grounds-keepers, electricians, public relations specialists, secretaries, physicians, dentists, wardens, etc, etc., etc.; I think you get the idea. One recent state police announcement listed positions with skills, and or experience in areas such as chemistry, accounting, counseling, foreign language, and aviators/pilot. The lists go on and on. How broad is your concept of criminal justice?

This brings us back to another consideration of your current role as student. National norms would suggest that from 20% - 30% of entering freshman classes are undecided regarding a major field of study. How about you? In addition, somewhere around 50% of all students will switch their major at least once. How about you? The issue is change. The most certain thing I can say on this topic is, change is and will be a permanent part of your educational and career experiences. This really is the underlying significance of Jeff's story. No matter how much you may resist, you and your circumstances will always be in motion. While it does not always seem that way, deep down we all realize this. For example, ask yourself, "Am I the person now that I want to be in 10 or 20 years?" If you answer no, to any degree, then you are on a path, which invites change. It is just that we do not typically think of it this way. But what about the person who says they are now the way they want to be in the next 10 to 20 years? Out of many responses I suggest two. One is, though you may resist it personally, change in circumstances is inevitable. It can be as near as experience with a disease or making a new friend, or as seemingly distant as the fluctuation of the Russian stock market or your wardrobe made in China or southeast Asia. The fact is you are connected in some way to all such movements in history. Therefore, the question is not whether you personally will change, but whether you will acknowledge this reality and then, with awareness, intentionally participate in your own future.

So, what does this mean for exploration in the field of criminal justice? Well it means several things. At your stage and station of life it would suggest at least two considerations. First, do not assume that you personally know, in any sufficient detail, what a specific career will hold for you. While you may want to go out and catch the bad guys, if you cannot accurately and clearly write the subsequent report, the bad guys may actually go free! It does happen. Or, you could end up like Jeff who spent an entire undergraduate and graduate education climbing on to the cutting edge of math; only to find that cross-cultural communication and understanding were his primary career needs at this time. The idea here is that your intended career has so much more breadth to it than you can possibly imagine. Be prepared to see the big picture.

The second consideration is to anticipate change, both personally and in your relevant environment. You may not always know the source or direction of some specific change movements, but you can at least assume that change is either just around the corner, or at least on the horizon. The juvenile gang roaming the streets today is the cell phone, pager and internet-linked organized crime machine of tomorrow. The fingerprint evidence of yesterday is the DNA trace today. The Jesse James bank robber of legend is the "computer-nerd-embezzler" laundering money through a maze of offshore banking systems. You must have an orientation, which makes you pliable, within limits, to real movement in your career. Otherwise, your career will move without you. If you do not yet believe the importance of such an orientation, then hear the words of my 77 year old father-in-law who answered the question, "What is the most significant invention of your lifetime?" with one word, "Electricity!" I wonder what will you say in 50 or 60 years?

Step 2: Reading the Rest of This Book

I hope that you actually get around to reading the Introduction to this book. In many instances the Introduction is overlooked as just some obligatory start to a text. I understand this and have therefore kept my introduction as brief and to the point as possible (perhaps you might already be saying, "Too late!"). Besides, you have a lot of other demands on your time; some worthy and others, should we say, not so worthy. Nevertheless, I understand this and seek to keep the momentum. But I do have a few things to say to you as you proceed to the rest of the book. Actually you may have already read some of the character profiles (or CP's as I refer to them) and are only now glancing through the Intro. In either case, I have something to say which I think will be helpful as you consider the CP's and your own future.

By now you should have concluded that the style of writing is less formal and more conversational. This is intentional for several purposes. First, this book is written for you, not my colleagues in research or distinguished scholars of criminal justice in colleges and universities. It is not full of overwhelming words or theories, just some important ideas. Second, you are exploring. You have not yet arrived. Therefore, I want anyone with an interest, or just curiosity, to have access to the material within. Third, the idea of a career just does not spring, full-blown, into anyone's mind. We often explore by talking over our own ideas with friends, family, and even the occasional professor. We look for information, guidance, validation, and approval. Unfortunately, in a book it is difficult to have an actual conversation. So, I try my best to anticipate your questions and to deal with them directly, and without confusing jargon. I want this, as much as possible, to be a conversation. We are talking about your future and that is a personal matter. I am trying to respect that with a personal style.

The main body of this book is a collection of character profiles (CP's). All CP's are accounts of real people as they have moved through a career in criminal justice. While the names have been changed and specific locales have been made more general for the reasons of privacy, do understand that the details are true to the experiences of the subjects who have shared their stories. The anonymity of the CP subject is necessary because of the full detail of their lives and careers, which they have provided.

The CP's will walk you through the professional lives of each subject. Included will be information about the origins of their interest in criminal justice, education and degrees earned, job history and career development, and where possible, income expectations. Special attention is given to what you, as students, could or should be doing now to prepare you for similar careers. In fact, it was the universal interest in students and your future in criminal justice, which was motivation enough for them to participate. You should understand that the only reward our CP subjects receive is the knowledge that they may have contributed to your future. No one was paid for his or her story, and they remain anonymous.

To make the most of your reading of the CP's consider the following. Understand that this book is not so much about criminal justice as it is about the lives of people whose careers have developed in the field of criminal justice. You can certainly learn something about policing, prosecuting, and corrections, but I would recommend attention to what the CP's say about the work. To this end I have some specific suggestions.

As you read, write questions or comments about career development in the margins. Don't just highlight or you will end up with whole pages highlighted! Think about the choices the people made. What kinds of skills do they have or wish they had? What kinds do they recommend you develop? What values and ideas do they promote, and why? What is the role of others in their lives? Who influenced them, positively or negatively, and what was the result? What is common of all CP's put together? In spite of the unique cases, is there a typical CP pattern? What are the lateral or transferable skills evidenced in each CP? Remember my challenge to discover how

4

composition, sociology and computer science, to name just a few, are related to law enforcement? Check that list again or better yet, develop one of your own for the value of other disciplines in the pursuit of criminal justice. In what ways have the CP's lives and careers changed over time?

Do not read anything into the order of the CP's as presented in the following chapters. They are simply a sampling of what is possible. My recommendation is to take a specific career not mentioned as a challenge to find out more. Research your own CP's, using these as a model. The CP's are also short. It is not my intent to tell you everything about a particular career, not because it wouldn't be interesting, but because this book would lack important breadth. Because the CP's are short and in no particular order, you are welcome to start reading at any point. Perhaps you have already done this. If so, you can now go back and build on your first encounters. Actually, I hope to present, in a user-friendly way, the fascinating field of career opportunities in criminal justice.

2

CHIEF OF POLICE

Chet Bennett, 55 years old, has been on a fast track for much of his career. Since 1980 he has served as Chief of Police for two departments, located within major west coast metropolitan areas. Chet is very clear about what it takes to be an effective law enforcement officer. He is also just as certain about the wrong reasons for which people enter the force. Chet's philosophy is evidenced in the idea of a mission statement for his department. As published, the statement reads:

MISSION

WITH PROFESSIONALISM, RESPECT, AND INTEGRITY, WE WILL MAINTAIN A PARTNERSHIP WITH THE COMMUNITY, STRIVING TO IMPROVE THE QUALITY OF LIFE BY PROVIDING A SAFE AND SECURE ENVIRONMENT FOR ALL.

ORGANIZATIONAL VALUES

PROFESSIONALISM

WE VALUE PROFESSIONALISM AND BEING ACCOUNTABLE TO THE HIGHEST STANDARDS OF LAW ENFORCEMENT. WE ENCOURAGE DEDICATION AND A STRONG COMMITMENT IN PROVIDING QUALITY SERVICE TO OUR COMMUNITY.

RESPECT

WE VALUE THE RIGHTS OF ALL PEOPLE, TREATING THEM IN A FAIR AND COURTEOUS MANNER, WITH AN EMPHASIS ON INDIVIDUAL DIGNITY AND WORTH.

INTEGRITY

WE VALUE TRUTHFULNESS AND HONESTY, AND CONSIDER THEM VITAL TO OUR ORGANIZATION. WE ARE COMMITTED TO ETHICAL CONDUCT BY ALL MEMBERS OF OUR DEPARTMENT, AND TO THE HIGHEST STANDARDS OF MORAL CHARACTER IN SERVING OUR COMMUNITY. WE ARE COMMITTED TO JUSTICE AND FAIRNESS, AND WILL ABIDE BY THE LAW ENFORCEMENT CODE OF ETHICS.

DEVELOPMENT OF EMPLOYEES

WE VALUE OUR EMPLOYEES AS OUR GREATEST ASSET. WE BELIEVE IN EMPOWERING INDIVIDUALS WHO REFLECT THE ORGANIZATION'S VALUES, THROUGH GREATER AUTONOMY AND CONTROL WITHIN THEIR SCOPE OF RESPONSIBILITY. WE ARE COMMITTED TO THE RECRUITMENT, DEVELOPMENT, AND RETENTION OF THE HIGHEST QUALITY EMPLOYEE AVAILABLE. WE ENCOURAGE AN ATMOSPHERE OF INNOVATION AND PROBLEM SOLVING, AND PROVIDING THE EQUIPMENT AND TECHNOLOGY NECESSARY TO ACCOMPLISH OUR MISSION.

EQUALS ***PRIDE

The reason for including this statement is to evidence the seriousness with which Chet takes the role of the police department in the community. Such a statement is not what most aspirants would think of in preparation for this career, or a specific law enforcement job. But it is what Chet thinks about, and is why he is so insistent on getting the best possible candidates for any job in the department. According to Chet, "If you are someone who is simply interested in wearing the badge, or you are impressed with the authority of the position, then you are absolutely not what I look for in an officer. If you have a 'bone to pick,' law enforcement is not for you. If you were on the wrong end of peer groups while growing up, and now in law enforcement you believe you have the opportunity to turn the tables, then, we have no place for you on our force. The characteristics I've just described are the very characteristics which result in a Rodney King beating." The point, according to Chet, is "We are here to provide service to our community. There cannot be any other agenda."

So, what was Chet's agenda? Actually there seem to be a variety of contributors to Chet's self-image as a person, as a law enforcement officer, and the work of a law enforcement agency. In the early 1960's Chet was in junior college with no real concept of a career. "What I was really interested is was commercial art. However, it really didn't seem possible to attend the right school for completing this kind of degree. While I still do art as a hobby, I'm not so sure that my situation was ever good enough to make it my career." In 1964 Chet was drafted and served in the Army reserves. He entered Officer Candidate School and received his commission as a Second Lieutenant. His reserve responsibility required 6 months active duty and two years total service. According to Chet, "I still had no idea of a career, and I knew that I would not be pursuing commercial art. I just worked at a variety of jobs until I was able to sort things out." That sorting was influenced by two different events.

"I had a younger brother who was constantly in trouble with the law, and detectives were always at the house. I actually got to know them. On a trip home while still in the reserves, one detective asked me what I was going to be doing after my discharge. I still really did not know." But this did get Chet to thinking about the possibilities. Later a friend in the reserves talked to him more specifically about police work. Chet knew military structure, and he had become an officer, so he had experiences compatible with the structure of law enforcement. "So," according to Chet, "I decided to give it a try." A local department was hiring so "I made an application and received a letter asking me to come in for a test. I was hired and enrolled in the police academy for eight weeks." Upon graduation from the academy Chet took a position with the department for the next six years. He also began an Associate's degree in Police Science, which he eventually completed in 1974. What he needed, and was about to get, was experience.

In 1972 Chet began to take a number of steps, which propelled him in eight years from patrolman to chief. Essentially, Chet's first promotion was a function of positions being available, the requisite training and experience, and successfully testing for the position. This all came together for Chet in 1972 and he was promoted to Sergeant. From 1972-1975, he was still on patrol. In 1975, he became Training Manager until 1977 (still a Sergeant's position). By this time Chet had developed a helpful perspective on his work and what it took to advance within it. "Basically, you must put your all into everything you do. You may be interested in a promotion, but you must do the job you are in first, not simply work at the promotion." His position as training manager put him more squarely into police administration. Among other things he processed newly hired officers and developed work schedules. According to Chet, "I liked this kind of work. It was an opportunity to influence the development of new officers, and through them the development of the department."

After two years as training manager Chet really began to accelerate his career in terms of movement up the departmental ladder. As circumstances developed there were promotional opportunities to both lieutenant and captain levels at a department in another city. The new chief there was trying to fill his executive staff positions and Chet received a letter inviting him to apply. According to Chet, "I had begun to see that there was opportunity ahead if I was both qualified and aggressive. So, I applied. After the testing and interviews I was selected for one of the two captains' positions." Basically, Chet skipped the lieutenant's rank.

At this time Chet was clearly on a path upward, but he still needed to put some of the puzzle pieces in place. His city manager advised him that the next level, the chief's position, required a four-year degree. So, he enrolled in a bachelor's program and earned a criminal justice degree in 1979. In 1980, the Chief of Chet's department retired. Chet, with three years of experience at the Captain's level was the logical choice for Acting Chief until the city council could organize a search for a new captain. According to Chet, "I attended the city council meeting with the expectation that I would be appointed Acting Chief. But as things turned out I was offered the job of Chief. It was surprising because I hadn't actually applied for the job."

For the next six years Chet worked as Chief, learning the variety of functions involved in that job. "You now have more people making demands on your work and time." These included, among other things, working with budget and personnel departments, city council members and the city manager, as well as setting policy for departmental operations. This latter point includes everything from hiring to training, scheduling, promotion, budgeting, etc. Responsibilities ranged from patrol officers, to animal control, the jail, and interagency relations. According to Chet, "The job really pulls you in a lot of different directions. For example, most people would not typically think of making speeches or writing grants and reports. It can be a very challenging job in terms of the variety of demands it makes on you."

In 1986, Chet applied for the Chief of Police position in another community. There were approximately 100 applicants, and Chet was selected and offered the position. When asked why he moved Chet answered, "I'd had my eye on that department for some time. What attracted me were a number of things. Overall the department and city is an excellent environment. The organization was in good shape, and it had solid financials. There was a sound philosophy and the department had a history of stability, with only two previous chiefs. Finally, the department had an excellent reputation, and I liked it."

From Chet's point of view his new department had an outstanding foundation. There was a productive history and culture. However, there were trends, which, if left unaddressed, could be problematic in the future. Among other things the city itself was evolving, and there was a need for more officers on the street. From Chet's perspective the department had one source of additional officers, and they were already on force. However, they were in jobs like records, animal control, the jail, and behind other desks. If they could somehow get those officers into the street then they would be able to address a growing need. But what to do about the jobs left behind? The answer, according to Chet, was, "civilianization." The idea is that if you have sworn officers in desk jobs then you are wasting resources. Put them in the field, which is what their training prepares them to do, and you can fill the non-hazardous or non-arrest duties with civilians, and at a lower cost. If you are going to invest so much in training and special benefits for sworn officers, then you should have them in positions where you need them the most. To accomplish this Chet enlisted the services of a consultant to make a plan and design a structure for the department. The result was a 10 year plan which, according to Chet, ". . . we have followed very closely." Of course, this has brought its own challenges, as you work to transition a traditional department. According to Chet, "You are not going to convince everyone of the correctness of this kind of move. Some people will just not be able to make the change. However, if you are willing to work with people you have a good chance of winning them over. The other thing is that we have a 10-year plan. This means that you will have an opportunity to develop new people as they come on board."

It is in this latter regard that Chet has specific and passionate points of view. "On the one hand," according to Chet, "I like to see students work at their education while they are also working on the force. The reason is that as you learn ideas and concepts you have the immediate opportunity to see how they apply." But, this is not always possible, and it is the case that more and more departments are looking for candidates with college degrees. So, what is it that Chet looks for in potential new officers? There are three broad categories of traits; personal qualities, skills, and education.

Regarding personal qualities Chet says, "It is imperative that our officers demonstrate honesty, integrity, and maturity. These are givens. Anything other than these undermines everything we try to do. Our work is with the citizens of this community, and they have to be able to have faith in us.

But there are other qualities. One of these is an openness to people from different social and cultural backgrounds. Our officers need to be open to all people, not just people like themselves. In our community we have white, black, Hispanic, and Asian populations throughout. If you have and tend to act on biases, then you will fail to do your job in an increasingly diverse world. Another vital quality is sensitivity or compassion. You have to be able to put yourself in the shoes of others, see what they see, and to an extent, feel what they feel. This is often quite lacking in most police departments. For example, in the case of a child's death by drowning, it is often the case that officers tend to the facts, as they should. However, officers should also tend to the parents involved. What are they feeling, what are they going through, what can the officers do to help with the next steps? Those are the kinds of things I mean by sensitivity."

Under the headings of skills and education Chet includes a variety of learned abilities or acquired perspectives, as well as formal courses of study. These are combined here because they both include a learning process. "It is important that officers have the quality of being well read. While this includes what you can learn from books, it also includes what you can learn from a variety of life experiences. Have you sampled a variety of what life has to offer, and have you learned from these experiences? Have you, for example, worked while growing up? What did that teach you? You need to be in good physical condition. There are two reasons for this. One is that some aspects of the job require it. Two, you are less likely to suffer from poor self-image associated with bad physical condition. While you are an officer, it is often the rank or position that the public sees, not you. How you present yourself to that pubic is important. Related is an awareness of the importance of a professional appearance. The public has an expectation of us, and how we appear to them helps in creating a necessary level of confidence. It is important that our officers have an ability to shape themselves into the environment. They need to understand the cultures and ways of the community. They must understand how to act, according to those cultures, and in different situations. Officers need to know how to communicate both verbally and nonverbally. Along these lines we have increasing needs for officers with language skills such as Spanish, Vietnamese, Taiwanese, and Chinese. In general, you need to know and understand people."

As far as courses of study are concerned, Chet says that really any major can be useful. But there are areas of coursework, which are especially impactful. According to Chet, "Perhaps the most important coursework to take is that which develops and hones your writing skills. 70% of your success in law enforcement will rely upon your ability to translate what you see and observe into a form, which clearly communicates to a very wide audience. An inability to do so will cause you to fail. Likewise, your ability to speak will greatly enhance or diminish your ability to get the job done. I am talking not only about an ability to communicate appropriately in situations on the street, but also in formal presentations. You will eventually be speaking before all kinds of groups, whether they are elementary school classes, the PTA, or courtroom testimony. You cannot be timid. You must have self-confidence. I used to get physically ill before a speech in school. It was bad, but now I don't even have a butterfly. It is just a necessary skill. Finally, take come course work in history and political science. The reason is that with history you get context. You need to have a feel for why things are done the way they are. In addition, you are an employee of government. You are a part of government. You need to know what the issues are and how governments work."

Finally, whatever else police work is, it is work with people. Police departments work for city governments, and for the citizens at large. Police officers also work with other officers and law enforcement agencies. Officers must know how to work in teams. And, officers must understand crime and criminals. What it comes down to is people and the skills you have in managing your relationships with them. This is especially critical for a department of about 200 officers and civilians. Salaries for the Chief's position in departments of this size in Chet's region range from $80,000-$120,000 annually.

In conclusion, Chet is a Chief of Police in a day and age of change and challenges. Officers must combine personal qualities of integrity with development of physical skills and an ability to communicate across cultures. While challenging and at times difficult or even depressing-- work of policing can certainly set you back on your heels--it is also highly rewarding and stimulating.

3

STATE'S ATTORNEY

Greg Samuelson, age 44, has served for approximately fifteen years in the role of State's Attorney. The more common term for this position is District Attorney (the "DA"). In function the State's Attorney is actually a prosecuting attorney. An elected position the State's Attorney prosecutes offenders, on behalf of the state. Depending on population the State's Attorney will make the state's case in prosecution of offenders from traffic violations and shoplifting to armed robbery and murder. The larger the district or county the greater the opportunity for specialization. The smaller the district or county the more the State's Attorney must be a generalist. Greg tends to operate as a generalist, occasionally calling on specialists for unique or technical cases.

Greg's college education and career, while related, did not constitute a seamless progression from interest to present role. After his freshman year Greg was drafted and spent two years on active military duty. He returned to school after his discharge and finished the next three years earning a BS degree in business. Immediately thereafter Greg spent one year working for an accounting firm and another year working for his Alma Mater as coordinator of cooperative education. According to Greg, " I began to develop interests in law school but thought that financial limitations would serve to keep me out. I really thought I'd probably end up somewhere in business management." However, after a couple of years of work Greg saw that law school could be an option and subsequently enrolled.

Critical to Greg's career were his summer internships. According to Greg, "Heading into law school I had some ideas of areas I might pursue. However, those were not especially limiting, so I was rather open to direction." That direction was given some definition during his first summer of law school. "I had developed a level of interest in the State's Attorney's role and had an opportunity to work in an office. I would have to say that I became quite interested, even fascinated with the work of the State's Attorney's office. Among other things there was a mix of courtroom and other duties. It was a varied work environment where I encountered new situations every day. It actually had a refreshing appeal."

In his second summer internship Greg was granted a "711" license which allowed him to appear in court. Among other things, "I was allowed to handle motions in felony cases. And I even tried a traffic case before a jury prior to having my degree." This of course was done under supervision of the State's Attorney and authorized by his "711" license. Greg found the work to be "quite enjoyable." In addition Greg was exposed to the political realities of the position. "I had always been somewhat interested in politics, and now I had a chance to see it up close. In fact, I participated in the 1980 campaign for re-election of my supervising State's Attorney. I learned how the local party worked and attended precinct meetings. I observed how the State's Attorney worked with others, how he put together support for projects, how skillful he was at lining people up." This working of interpersonal relationships was not only an official part of the job, but an unofficial part of the work, outside the job. For example, regarding decision-making Greg relates, "When a decision is made by a board and reported we need to understand that there is always a history to that decision and how it developed. It did not just somehow and suddenly occur." With such an understanding, for example, about county board decisions, you are in a better position to "sell" or at least explain what was done. "I learned that relationships were critical to any job I might have in law enforcement."

In 1981 Greg graduated from law school and went to work part-time with the same State's Attorney's office in which he had interned. He also worked part-time in private practice. In late 1981 Greg earned his license to practice law. For a while Greg simply continued to learn the practice of law. Then, in 1983 the State's Attorney in his office was appointed to a judgeship. Greg, by virtue of his experience in that office, and his current part-time status, was the logical choice for appointment to complete the term of the departing State's Attorney. Greg's previous political work on behalf of the State's Attorney certainly facilitated his appointment since by law the appointment, made by the county board, had to be made within the incumbent party and with the party's endorsement. Since then, Greg has won election and re-election as State's Attorney in 1984, 1988, 1992, and 1996.

Now as the State's Attorney Greg developed a new perspective on the job. According to Greg, "The decisions I used to make and send to my boss for consideration were actually recommendations. Now the decisions were mine alone. The reality and difficulty of this is that decisions have to be made and we all have to live with them. Before, I simply had to make good and sound recommendations, now I was feeling the weight of responsible decisions." This weightiness was especially evident when considering the circumstances of the victim. According to Greg, "The State's Attorney's job is one in which decisions are and must be made, and they must be made within some time frame. You cannot rewind the clock and decide again. Furthermore, the victim cannot also rewind the clock. No matter what, you will never make the victim whole or fully satisfied. Likewise, you have to understand that the person prosecuted may also have family, friends, and work. In doing your job you could easily destroy a large part of various people's lives. At the conclusion of things, you solve only part of the victim's problems and create new ones for the family of the criminal. No one is completely happy."

As an elected official Greg realizes that nearly everyone will have a specific opinion about his work. Furthermore, according to Greg, many in the electorate feel it is their right and duty to talk with and advise him on his decisions. This can be quite frustrating, but at the same time necessary and even useful. "The problem is no situation is simply black or white. It is always some shade of gray. Many people don't understand this and become upset, for example, if I don't choose to prosecute to

13

the fullest extent of the law. But this point of view, whatever it is, does constitute a part of the community within which the crime occurred, and within which it must ultimately be resolved. Therefore, such information and points of view constitute the necessary history that a two-page police report simply cannot capture. You must somehow come to know the parties involved, their history, and not just a slice in time."

One of the most sensitive issues in the work of a State's Attorney is sentencing. Again, the problem is that every circumstance is different, and none of them are simply black and white in their clarity. According to Greg, "Sentencing depends on the seriousness of the crime, the state established framework for range of sentences, criteria such as the history of the criminal, the cost of incarceration, the interest of the victim, and whether the sentence is designed as punishment to the criminal, deterrence of others, restitution, etc." Sentencing is a balancing act. Complicating the scenario are the tendencies of local jurors and presiding judges.

If sentencing is most sensitive then plea-bargaining is most controversial. In part, it is a problem of perception. According to Greg, it is an administrative and fiscal necessity. The problem is when the practice becomes politicized. Here is the reality. In Greg's jurisdiction, which is not large, there has been an annual average of about 100 felonies, 200 misdemeanors, and 1500 traffic cases. Further, out of a recent pool of 150 jurors 93 were immediately excused for various personal reasons. This is before the lawyers begin to select. As Greg says, "It is becoming increasingly difficult to find hard working individuals willing to serve as jurors." Given this situation is it reasonable to expect jury trials in all cases? "The task," according to Greg, " is to find the middle ground." That middle ground may include the following considerations. While a jury trial may indeed result in a stiffer definition of guilt and sentence, the process may also result in pain and/or embarrassment for the victim and their family. Some victims just want immediate closure, and their rights bear respect. Some cases are politically charged and can consume an entire community (or country for that matter: i.e., O.J. Simpson). Plea bargains can avoid the creation of a spectacle. Finally, according to Greg, "No one should be so arrogant as to believe that there is a case you can't possibly lose. You can lose any case, and the plea bargain can guarantee a conviction on at least part of the charge." The key is whether the plea bargain fits the case. According to Greg, "Over the years you develop a sense of what the accused, the victim, and the community will accept. So, it's not just some blind shot in the dark."

Aside from criminal cases there are civil court responsibilities. Most State's Attorneys are required to represent the government body with which they are affiliated; in the case of Greg, the county board. This means he represents all board members and actions of the board to fulfill specific roles and duties. Included also are officials of the court and those who work for them. This can be quite difficult due to the complexity of both criminal and civil law.

One major consideration in the work of a State's Attorney is the state legislature. According to Greg, "The legislature deals with problems by passing laws. Now, the legislature's solution becomes my problem because the solution is often so impractical that it can't realistically be enforced. And, enforcement, particularly the use of fines, is not always practical." As an example, driving without insurance results in a fine of $500 and court costs of $250. How can we expect those who could not

14

afford to pay for insurance to both insure their cars and pay the fine? One "solution" is to pay the fine and court costs off at only $5.00 per month. But then it is necessary to have an office collect and account for hundreds and even thousands of such payments. It probably costs the jurisdiction more than $5.00 to collect $5.00.

A related issue is the shear number of laws. According to Greg, "The 1981 revised statutes took five volumes to print. The 1996 revised statutes took seven volumes, and with smaller print!" While laws are added, they are infrequently repealed. According to Greg, "Two to three new laws of consequence are passed each year, but we sometimes don't even receive the printed notice until after the effective date." The problem is that the legislature begins to micro-manage. There must be room for discretion, as in the choice of the policeman to give a ticket or just a warning.

For those considering a career such as State's Attorney it should be understood that variety and change must be addressed. You must assume that things will not stay the same. And, the vehicle for this variety and change is others--citizens, boards, criminals, victims, legislatures, businesses, etc., etc., etc. Therefore, people skills are preeminent. Remember also, this is an elected position. You have to answer to all kinds of constituencies, and be able to respond to a variety of movements and trends in society. Even now there are trends in progress. These include, but are certainly not limited to truth in sentencing and determinant sentencing (based on "get tough on criminal" legislatures), overcrowding of prisons, electronic monitoring, privatization of corrections, conflicting laws, the reach of crime into unsuspecting communities, and the diversifying of populations along ethnic and racial lines. All of these must be understood in the context of competing interests, even within the broad system of criminal justice--Judges, States Attorneys, Police, and Corrections.

As State's Attorney how can you prepare for such a moving target? Greg has some suggestions. You of course must finish a law school degree, and to do this Greg recommends undergraduate business and English courses. So much of the law is related to business, and writing is so much a part of law school that the two combined help to "get you through." According to Greg, "All law school is communication in writing, with business, taxation, and government the usual topics. You must at least be familiar with general business concepts, such as accounting, in order to make it." But getting through law school and working out as a successful State's Attorney are two different things. The key here, according to Greg, is the internship. It is in the internship that you learn how to work with the people involved. As Greg says, "It's a human system."

Finally, it is possible to make a descent living. By state salary schedule Greg earns $71,500 annually, plus benefits. Depending on the cost of living locally that figure will vary somewhat.

4

SMALL TOWN POLICE OFFICER

Sergeant Jennifer Mykonos, now 43, did not really get started on her present career path until age 33. Prior to that she was raising two children at home, and feeling a bit restless about what to do. "I had graduated from high school in the early 70's. And while I think I always had a desire for work in law enforcement the opportunities for me just weren't there yet." Then one day she saw a job advertisement in a local newspaper for a police officer. She answered the ad and applied. "I passed the physical test, but I really didn't have enough of a background then to have much of a chance at being hired. But on a good note, I did meet some people and the experience helped me focus my attention more on what I wanted to do." As a result, Jennifer enrolled in an Administration of Justice program at the local community college. "Among other things I completed a 240 hour internship with the same police department where I had first applied. It was a very good experience, as I was able to do everything but arrest. I patrolled with the officers, went on all kinds of calls, did PR at various public events, like fairs and with local schools. I even had a chance to guard a celebrity on a visit to town. The result of this experience was a cementing of what I really wanted to do."

The degree and the internship have paid dividends in a variety of ways. As mentioned above, Jennifer said her first application gave her the opportunity to meet people. The internship maximized this opportunity. "When it comes right down to it, police work is all about working with people; your fellow officers and the public generally. I made some good friends on that internship, and they in turn helped me on my way." That help was manifested in a departmental sponsorship of Jennifer for the Police Academy. What this did was get Jennifer on to the next stage of her career. However, there was no commitment on the part of the sponsoring department to hire her upon graduation. According to Jennifer, "In some ways this was a really unusual arrangement. The Chief was not obligated to do this, but I am obviously grateful that he did."

The academy experience was both challenging and rewarding. According to Jennifer, "It was 10 weeks of long days, from 6:00 a.m. to 5:00 p.m. We focused on three general areas; lots of classroom study, firearms training, and physical testing." In the classroom a wide array of topics were covered. Much time was given to lectures and study of criminal law, in particular the state's vehicle code. According to Jennifer, "While it certainly is not all that you do, paying attention to and monitoring traffic is a significant part of what we do. But a traffic stop is so much more than simply

16

enforcing the law. You are also interacting with the public. So, we also took coursework on how to approach and speak with people, deal with the elderly and handle juveniles, to name just some. Each category of people generally requires different kinds of treatment or approaches." All of this should be understood in light of the fact that wherever Jennifer went, she was typically the first and only female involved. While at the Academy, Jennifer was one of two women in a total class of 30. According to Jennifer, "I experienced no real gender problem. They seemed rather accepting. If they did have problems with me, I didn't notice or know about it."

When Jennifer graduated from the Academy she was on her way in law enforcement, and in a state of limbo. Because of her sponsorship arrangement, and the fact that she was not graduating to a specific job, she was not able to take the state certification exam for police officers. In fact, she was out of the Academy and not working for about seven months when she learned that a nearby town of about 1,800 was in need of a part-time officer. "That job was a real benefit to me. The people there actually worked it out so that I was able to work full-time. Also, because I had a job, I was able to take and pass the certification exam. It really was an excellent way to start out. In a small town everyone knows everyone else and you have to learn to put in practice what they have tried to teach you in college and the Academy. It was a rather low key setting in which to get started."

After 1-½ years on the job the department, which originally sponsored Jennifer, was again hiring, and she again made application, going through all the testing and interviews. She was ranked first among the applicants and was offered the position. It was September of 1990, and Jennifer was the first woman hired in that department. Now in her ninth year Jennifer feels that she has thoroughly adapted to her work situation regarding gender. However, she admits, "When I first came into the department I was somewhat afraid that the gender issue might be a problem. But I have to say, as far as my working relationship within the department, I have had no problems at all. I can't vouch for what the other offices may had said in private, or what they thought at first, but in their work with me, they have been very professional."

Actually, the more significant challenge has been relationships with the public. According to Jennifer, "While this town is larger than the one I first worked in, it is still a small town. People here can be rather traditional and the fact of a female officer was just not part of their experience. It wasn't a hostile environment, but it was challenging. I realized that I not only had to be a police officer, but I had to be sensitive to how people saw me. It was up to me to somehow win them over. One of my earliest experiences was a call to unlock a car. An elderly woman had locked her keys inside. When I got there and went about unlocking the car the lady asked what I was doing? She just didn't expect me to be women, and she was not fully comfortable with me. However, after that she later called the department for another reason and asked specifically for me. In fact, this is how it has often worked for me. Initial reactions ranged from resistance to some stronger emotions. My job was to somehow sell them on the idea that I am a capable and qualified law enforcement officer. While it still occasionally is brought up in some situations, I would have to say that after 9 years, it really has diminished."

This does not mean that gender issues are no longer relevant. According to Jennifer, "Women have to prove themselves each time out. The challenge is always there." But there were specific ways

17

that she and her department set about to meet that challenge. "I took training as a DARE officer and this then got me into the city's school system on a regular basis. As a result kids I'd meet in school would often recognize me on the street. They felt as if I were approachable. They simply knew me as a police officer. I also did PR by speaking in high school and college classes."

There do appear to be circumstances in which gender does impact police work. "For example there is a perception on the part of the public that there are situations that women can handle better. A case in point would be dealing with the victim of a rape. While this may not always be the case, if the victim believes things will be better with a female officer then I'm glad to help. There is also a feeling, or assumption, that women have a calming effect on the emotions. This may again be the perception of the public, but if it works then we should use it to our advantage. It is my opinion that men and women have their strengths, and we need both kinds in a police force." One particular situation, which detractors often raise, is the confrontation with a larger and stronger subject. According to Jennifer, "Sometimes the big burly guys are less likely to act up or take threatening steps because they do not perceive me as a threat. What is really important in this, and all cases, is to be smart and use common sense. You are always better off if you can talk your way out of a potentially bad situation instead of having to use physical force, or your firearm."

Since joining the force in 1990, Jennifer has developed as an officer in a number of different ways. She has had formal training in homicide investigations, forensics, securing crime scenes, photography, working with the elderly, interview techniques, creating composite identifications, defensive driving, and techniques of administering pepper spray, to name some. According to Jennifer, "The fact is you have to keep learning in this kind of work. Society is always changing, and you have to do your best to keep up. If you are not prepared to continue training, or if you don't believe it is necessary then don't get into this line of work."

While formal training is certainly part of the law enforcement officer's career, Jennifer suggests that " . . . it is also important to keep learning from experience. One thing you realize soon after you first start out is that the situations which are so easily 'black and white' in the academy are not so clear in real life. You find out that every situation is unique, and you have to treat every situation that way. In order to do this you have to use your judgment. This is really important because what you decide can have lasting effects on the people involved. Related to this is the fact that in so many situations you may have only seconds to decide. It's a heavy responsibility, that in seconds you can affect another person for the rest of their life." One other lesson of experience is empathy; "You have to be able to see a situation from the other person's point of view. This gets back to the fact that all situations are unique."

By 1996, Jennifer was ready to move on in her career. With promotional openings becoming available she decided to apply and test for Sergeant. Essentially she had to test before a board of police commissioners and chiefs. She had to prepare a written report and make an oral presentation on some matter relevant to the department. In her case Jennifer prepared a project proposal for improving departmental scheduling. In addition she had to submit to a psychological evaluation. Ultimately the board decided, and in November of 1996 Jennifer became Sergeant Mykonos. "I still patrol, but I also have more administration responsibilities. One way of looking at this is, it is my job to make and keep the other officers happy. You do this with reasonable scheduling, inspections, helpful performance reviews, development of training opportunities, and an empathetic style. You have to work with your other officers, not just order them around. You must also mentor new officers. I have to remember what it was like to be new myself. I try to keep an eye on them, but without them really knowing it. I don't want them feeling as if I'm always looking over their shoulders. They have to grow and mature, just as I did."

Jennifer believes there are several critical characteristics or orientations to the job, which potential law enforcement officers need to understand. "You must have, and be able to use common sense. Each situation, besides being unique, is also composed of a lot of different aspects, and you have to be able to see the connections. The problem is that a lot of people simply do not have it (common sense). Verbal skills are absolutely necessary. It is a skill, which allows you to get inside another person, see things from their point of view, and even defuse a potentially explosive situation. And, you have to be able to use this skill quickly, and maybe in just a minute or two, or even seconds in some cases. Your words can immediately make a situation better or worse. You have to have creativity and ingenuity. Part of your job is to solve another person's problem. These problems come in all shapes and sizes. But you have to remember, what may be a simple or small problem to you, can be an enormous problem to someone else. Finally, you have to be able to weather all the negative emotions. You will most likely be insulted, told that you are hated, or even attacked. If you cannot let that kind of stuff just roll you back, if you hold on to every insult, then this is not the job for you. In most cases it gets back to empathy. Many situations cause people to be quite emotional and they will often say one thing now, and apologize for it later. Still others just hate the uniform. So it's not really you, but what you represent. These kinds of things really bothered me at first, but I've learned to adapt."

Jennifer wants you to know that law enforcement is a rewarding career. But you must be clear-eyed about it. It is not as it generally appears on TV and in the movies. Your work can take you from crossing guard, to flooded basements, to squirrels in the attic, to bodies floating in the stream, or informing loved ones of an accidental death. This variety calls for a range of skills and perspectives. Jennifer offers some suggestions for students contemplating a career like hers. "You must be able to work in teams. You cannot do this job alone. Critical to this is honesty within the team and confidence in your team members. These characteristics reach to other law enforcement agencies and the public at large. Honesty is especially important in your relationship to state's attorneys and judges. Consistency in honesty results in respect. Respect produces a cooperative relationship and gives you standing in the community." Jennifer wants to make sure that future officers are also aware that, "There is a lot of writing. So, take composition classes, even grammar. The report is so important to success in your work. One mentor of mine said that the pen could be your most important weapon. An outsider must be able to read your report and be clear about what happened." Be prepared for a stressful schedule. "The schedule," according to Jennifer, "Can really be draining and a drag on your family. Carefully consider this as you try to combine family and career." Finally, Jennifer warns, "Do not get into law enforcement for the money." In her rural setting the salaries are rather low. Line officers earn in the low $20's. Jennifer earns approximately $26,000 plus benefits. However, according to Jennifer, "If you like people, then this is a job for you."

5

FEDERAL BUREAU OF INVESTIGATION

Nate Fredrickson is currently a special agent of the FBI. The title of special agent refers to those involved in active investigations of federal law violations. Now 55 years old, Nate has been with the FBI since 1969. According to Nate, "The FBI has high standards, demands quality, and is highly professional as an organization designed to fight crime." For those who aspire to the FBI Nate recommends, "Don't be lax in your attitude, attentiveness, and even your appearance. Be professional." For most this requires a substantial learning process which includes an undergraduate degree and relevant experience.

In Nate's case he was attending a small liberal arts college, majoring in business administration, when it became necessary to get a job to pay the bills. The local police department had positions open and Nate was hired. He worked there as an officer for the last two years of college and one additional year after graduation. While Nate learned the basics of law enforcement at the local police department level, the people he met on the job determined his future. In that community there was an office of the FBI. Over the years Nate came into contact with the agents there as they occasionally worked on cases together. According to Nate, "What began as simple contacts eventually turned into friendships. Friendships laid the groundwork for really understanding how the FBI worked. I developed a healthy respect for them as individuals, and the FBI as an organization. To me, they were the best in quality, and the best in pay."

It is important to understand a critical lesson about career development as illustrated by Nate's experience. Whether you begin with clear goals and a well-devised plan, or your decisions are made by necessity and your future is somewhat fuzzy, it still matters *who* you meet in life. This is not to say that intelligence, talent, and merit count for nothing. But it is to say that merit must be matched with opportunity for there to be an inkling of career. Opportunity is almost purely social. It does not just appear. It is created or presented by means of others. Because of this relationships are essential. They are the means and structures by which opportunities are distributed. So, *who* knows you, and *how* they know you, will significantly influence the opportunities and choices you will have to make. It is on these building blocks that a career can be launched.

Because of the relationships Nate had while serving on the local police force, he had the opportunity to see enough of the FBI to decide that his future, his immediate future as least, lay there. He made an application and waited on the Bureau's background check. On approval Nate was admitted in February of 1969 to the FBI training academy in Quantico, Virginia. In May of 1969, he graduated and was ready for his first assignment. But what did he learn while at the academy? There were at least three lessons. One was physical, a second was intellectual, and the third was social. The physical training in many respects was rather straightforward, though it did require discipline. The intellectual was more challenging. You must understand the law and the Bureau's place within it. Because of the litigious nature of society you must be sure of where you stand. The social lesson was the way the Bureau actually works. It is the culture and community of the FBI that ultimately makes it work. According to Nate, "As a part of the FBI you are a member of a tight-knit organization. It is really like an extended community. You are part of a network of people who associate in particular ways. We have a common language, common experiences, and a common culture. This really is very important because you must count on each other to do the job."

After graduating from the academy, Nate took a one-year probationary assignment. "It was there that I had to somehow put into practice the lessons of the academy. While I was a special agent I was also very lacking in experience. I really spent the year learning. Specifically, I spent time with an experienced agent learning that culture which they tried to teach us in the academy. Above all else I learned that as agents we all needed each other, all the time. Collaboration was the word."

From a probationary assignment in the Deep South Nate was transferred to an intensely urban assignment in the northeast. While there for the next seven years Nate's learning curve escalated dramatically. According to Nate, in his second assignment, "There was definitely a focus on violent crime. I was assigned to various squads which specialized in the pursuit of fugitives, kidnapping, extortion, and bank robbery. In a large department like that one you could afford to specialize. I also had the opportunity for additional training such as SWAT and anti-sniper tactics. Being in an urban area you also had to learn street survival." Each area of expertise required specific training. However, according to Nate, "The most significant details and largest amount of learning took place in the field. You could go back to the academy all you want for laboratory-like training in something such as an anti-sniper protocol. But not until you actually experience something like a sniper situation do you really figure out what needs to be done. And, what you find out is that you must rely on your peers. They teach you, and you in turn work with them."

Since 1978 Nate has been assigned to the same moderately sized metropolitan area agency. While it is urban, it is less intensely so, and it includes some rural areas within it. Nate is part of what is called an RA, or resident agency. A regional headquarters might contain up to 59 field officers. There are, however, fiscal pressures on the FBI to do more and more with less and less. The RA is one of the Bureau's answers to fiscal pressures for efficiency. The RA can range in size from one to eight agents with staffing such as a supervisor, secretary, and finance auditor. Rather than specializing in squads like those mentioned earlier, "We take pretty much what comes in the door," according to Nate. "We are much more the generalist."

Specialization has the advantage of expertise in some relatively small domain. But in fact, crime is rarely so specific. There is typically a lot of collateral involvement and damage. For example, a fugitive is more than someone just tying to stay out of the reach of the law. He typically has violated a host of other laws and involved a number of other people (i.e., stealing a car or taking a hostage). The other thing is that many crimes are multi-jurisdictional. They are such not only geographically, for example the crossing of state lines, but also in the spheres of responsibility, as in the case of a bank robbery. "This puts a premium on your relational skills," according to Nate. "If you cannot figure out how to get along with the local police officer who was first on the scene, then you will not make much progress in solving that particular crime." The fact is, we all tend to be somewhat territorial. We have 'turf' to protect. "The FBI agent must sort out competing interests in order to successfully, and efficiently, produce the desired conclusion to a crime situation." Typically the local police officers are first upon a crime scene. Depending on the nature of the crime the state police may be called in. In particular, local departments may need the crime scene investigation expertise the state police have. According to Nate, "If the crime falls within the interest or domain of the FBI then I must step in, but carefully. I usually rely at this point rather heavily upon the state police investigators because of their speed and expertise." After the crime scene investigation then certain lab experts take over. According to Nate, at this point the local police become generally less involved and the FBI role increases. "It really is a balancing act. You are almost always working with law enforcement officers over whom you have no authority. You have to be skilled at persuasion. But in order to be successful at this you must first have a relational foundation. You need regular contact with all personnel in the chain. Actually, it is a network of personal contacts. The personal relationship is the law enforcement relationship. You must be especially careful of not appearing to be coming in and taking over. You need everyone's input, and it is amazing how much harm you can do to an investigation by offending, inadvertently or not, someone along the way." Having been a local police officer for three years has perhaps made Nate more sensitive to this than many others. Essentially, the FBI functions on the receipt of information from a variety of sources. Therefore, the special agent cultivates any and all possible sources. This is just one reason why productive people skills are so important. "Our primary job," according to Nate, "is to solve crimes and put criminals in jail. To do this we depend greatly on others."

"Eventually," according to Nate, "we must make decisions as to what we can successfully pursue. More specifically, we must decide what we can prosecute. Sometimes you, as an agent, believe in the merits of your case. Yet the U.S. attorney's office decides the other way. You see, they have different criteria. They must figure whether they can make the case and get a conviction. If not, then we must move on. This can be very difficult to deal with at times, especially for local police who may be emotionally invested in a case. In my situation, I must think that if a case cannot be reasonably pursued then I'm better off dropping it and moving on to other cases. Otherwise, I am endlessly pursuing an unwinable case. Ultimately, I need to prioritize crime."

There is one final item which significantly impacts the FBI's mission. It is the rather unglamorous function of budgets. As has already been indicated, large regional offices with many specialists are necessarily giving way to Resident Agencies with generalists, who in turn must negotiate complex jurisdictional boundaries and parochial interests. In Nate's case, his RA, with eight agents, is responsible for five counties.

For those thinking of pursuing the career possibilities of the FBI, Nate has some rather specific advice. The basic criteria include a four year college degree, with any major, being less than 37 at time of appointment and mandatory retirement at 57. You should also have three years of employment history. Understand, all of this will be investigated in a background check, so it really matters the kind of personal history you are now creating. In this regard, Nate emphasizes a "clean lifestyle," right now. Begin making good lifestyle choices, right now. Understand that you are creating life patterns which will make a difference later in your life.

One such choice is a major area of study. Nate does not recommend criminal justice per se. In fact, Nate says, "A C.J. degree will not help at all. You must still make it in the FBI, and this means getting through the academy and being socialized into the FBI culture." So, Nate recommends majors like law, accounting, language, and the sciences. In addition students must excel at various forms of communication, both written and oral, as well as have a keen understanding of interpersonal relationships.

If you make the right choices and are in a position to start your career in criminal justice, Nate wants it understood that successfully fighting crime is very satisfying. And, it can be financially rewarding. Today salaries range form approximately $30,000 per year at step one, to the mid $60's at step 10. Overtime is possible and the benefits are substantial. But so are the personal benefits of a career in the FBI. "Fighting crime and helping people is ultimately rewarding."

6

PRISON WARDEN

Robert Walker is a warden in a federal correctional institution (FCI), part of the Federal Bureau of Prisons. Now in his late 40's, Rob has had a varied educational and career path which has prepared him broadly for the modern challenges of administering FCI's. In essence, an FCI is a small city. According to Rob, "Students should understand that all persons who work within an FCI are trained as correctional officers. But there is a wide array of actual job titles, from unit manager to cook, from guard to administrator in prison industries." The fact is, work in the Bureau of Prisons is not narrowly defined.

Rob graduated in 1970 with a degree in business administration and an emphasis in community analysis. Combining sociology and business Rob studied city management and public administration. Rob then enrolled in a Master's in Public Administration graduate program. According to Rob, "In the master's program I began to sort through my interests, deciding on government and law enforcement. I later narrowed this further to criminal justice."

Upon graduation in 1972 Rob worked for a year as a research associate in criminal justice. His work gave him access to a variety of criminal justice agencies. It was here that Rob's interests began to crystallize. After a short stint in the military Rob returned to graduate school where he earned his Ph.D. in public administration and continued working at the research center there. His focus again was criminal justice, and his work brought him in contact with still more agencies. Specifically Rob became interested in and learned more about corrections. Rob further began to establish a network of contacts, which were to become important to him as his career in corrections developed.

In 1975 Rob completed his Ph.D. and immediately went to work for the Bureau of Prisons. But why corrections? According to Rob, "There are actually a variety of reasons. Corrections offers one of the most unique and challenging management opportunities. It is never boring. The issues are so diverse, whether it is safety, utilities, infrastructure, or grounds, to name just some. From my point of view, it was a unique career, one which even had a 'mystique'."

Rob's first job with the Bureau was actually a transition position from his work in research. For about six months he continued as a researcher studying halfway houses. However, according to Rob,

"What I wanted was to work in prisons. I wanted basic line experience." This desire led to his first prison job as a case manager. It was certainly a time and opportunity for learning. According to Rob, "I had studied a lot of the issues, but had no experience with the offenders. I knew that I didn't know and needed to learn a lot. So, I adopted a learning posture. What is critical is that you have to learn how your personality and style of management will fit into that particular environment. There are no fixed styles for success, so you should not just copy someone else. You need to figure out what works for you. Most importantly," according to Rob, "is that I learned the value of interpersonal skills. Too often poor communications skills interfere with your work. Other priority skills include flexibility, adaptability, and not jumping to conclusions." You must in Rob's words, "Start to think."

After about eighteen months Rob moved on to unit manager. Rob was spending more time managing people, and this responsibility broadened considerably. In addition, Rob began to see the prison and the Bureau as more of an organization. The fact is that the prison is a collection of people " . . . moving in various directions and at different speeds." In light of this realization and his experience, Rob suggests students considering a career in corrections need to understand the details of organizational life, particularly one subject to the bureaucracy of the Federal government. In terms of promotion within such a system Rob notes that, " . . . upward mobility benefits from being visible in a positive way. This means that you must reach outside the immediate responsibilities. Take lateral responsibilities in order to experience other things. However, in each job you do, do it to completion. You cannot do so if you are looking ahead to your next promotion."

Rob's next career step was a move to Leavenworth, where for two years he served as the Executive Assistant to the Warden. According to Rob, "This was quite a different kind of institution for me. I went from an experimental to a more traditional environment." At Leavenworth Rob learned the benefits of routine, consistency and stability. But he was also there to implement change. Rob's assignment was to introduce unit management, which was a more departmental system of organization. This was a Bureau mandate, but that does not make change necessarily easy. In fact, change efforts usually produce resistance at first. Success is dependent not on the mandate of authority, but upon interpersonal skills and the ability to successfully sell the changes to those most affected. More and more Rob was experiencing the prison as an organization with multiple interests, responsibilities, trends and movements. This latter point was becoming more critical to Rob as he took on a new position with the Bureau, this time outside of prison-specific work. Rob was now Director of the Staff Training Center for the Bureau of Prisons. The obvious task is the dissemination of information and training of personnel. But more than this, according to Rob, "We tried to pass on the history, traditions, and the mind of the Bureau of Prisons. In other words, the culture of the organization." The intended objective was a new "professionalism."

From staff training, Rob next moved to the position of Warden at a prison camp. The camp is actually a support structure for the operation of an FCI. Such camps are usually smaller, house minimum security prisoners, and typically have no walls. According to Rob, "I really wasn't ready for the CEO job. I had moved rather quickly through the ranks, and not all my time had been spent in actual prisons. So much of prison work is people management that only experience can really teach you what you need to know." A particular issue here is change. The role and function of prisons in America have frequently shifted over the decades. Prisons have variously been charged to rehabilitate, punish, or simply protect society. With each of these have come different programs, different emphases, and variations in resources, including budgets. In many cases the same personnel have experienced all such initiatives. According to Rob, "What is critical is that whatever change is necessary the staff must ultimately have ownership. Otherwise, the change will not take effect."

The variety of positions held by Rob were preparing him ultimately for that CEO position he claimed not to be ready for earlier in his career. However, before that he had other major assignments. He developed and was the first director of the National Academy of Corrections. This institution serves as a kind of graduate school for federal, state, and local correctional personnel. Those who attend the Academy are in effect on sabbatical from work. There they can take the time necessary to evaluate programs, jails, and prisons, and see how these fit into local communities. Here the issues included working relationships with persons such as elected officials and city planners. The critical idea is that prisons do not operate in isolation, they operate in some context. Knowing this prepares future wardens for their jobs.

That job, in Rob's case, was warden of a new FCI. According to Rob, "This was a unique challenge. Among other things, as a new institution we had no history or traditions. A sense of who you are is important to what you do, but here we did not have that. The entire staff was put together from local hires and transfers. As such, this was a real, yet gratifying challenge." Because of such challenges,
"Wardens today need new skills in order to be successful. Specifically, the job of the Warden is so much more externally oriented than in the past. There are more externally generated influences and pressures than in the past and these include tax payers and elected officials. We find that such constituents are less tolerant of mistakes or errors. For these and other reasons Wardens who have been good at managing the internal environment now must learn to assess external pressures. However, more than just answering the questions and concerns of local constituents, Wardens must now proactively engage the local community." It is in this capacity that Rob continues to this day, developing the history and traditions of a new FCI.

Perhaps you are thinking about a career in Federal Corrections, but you are wondering what you, as a student, should be doing? First of all you should know that there are over 200 job categories and over 80 work locations around the U.S. There are some specific requirements such as being under 37 years of age at the time of your first job. An excellent resource for all such information is the Federal Bureau of Prisons' employment internet site. Its address is *www.bop.gov*. Here you will see specific job announcements, including qualifications and salary ranges, which exceed $100,000 per year. But still, what should you do, right now as a student?

According to Rob, what you do depends at least somewhat on what you envision for yourself within the field of corrections. The field had become much more competitive in recent years. Because of this you should take any opportunity to gain experience while in school. Networking is still critical to career development and experience, such as internships are invaluable. This means that people today choosing correctional careers are, increasingly, those who are preparing for it. Vanishing from the landscape are those people simply experimenting with corrections as one among several career options. This does not mean that an absolutely specific academic preparation is required. According to Rob there is room and need for persons with both degrees in criminal justice as well as degrees in a wide variety of other disciplines. However, one common thread is either a degree or substantial coursework in the social sciences.

This latter point is critical in that the most important skill mentioned by Rob is interpersonal skill. "You must be able to engage others in a meaningful and productive way. If you cannot, or do not understand how to do this, then work in corrections is virtually impossible. You must understand that persons in a prison setting, prisoners and staff alike, come from a wide variety of backgrounds. Therefore an interpersonal skill which works in one situation may be inappropriate in another. While in school you should take advantage of any opportunity to deal with a wide variety of people, to engage in cross-cultural opportunities. You will quickly learn that you must keep an open mind, be willing to adapt, and perhaps most importantly, listen."

7

THE CORONER

Dan Alger has been a county coroner in an urban setting for fourteen years. Before that he served as investigator for a State's Attorney for four years, and for thirteen years was an officer in a city police department. According to Dan, "The position of coroner is political in that it is an elected office. Depending on the county, the office may be very political or not so political. You might not think of someone dying as being so charged with political overtones, but death does not occur in a vacuum. A particular death is a fact. How we interpret that death is the politics of it." Dan became a candidate for coroner at the request of county Democrats. Up until his election the coroner had been in Republican hands for 36 years, and had been the only non-Democratic office in that particular county. So, in a real sense, it was a political consideration that moved Dan into this role.

Dan sees his role as that of an investigator. "As a coroner it is my job to explain why someone died. We use any means at our disposal to accomplish this goal. Because of this I see death investigation as a pyramid; it has a very broad base and narrows to a conclusion. For example, you may learn more by examining the room in which a death occurred than you would by examining the body. You must be open to any kind of input. This is not a job for the narrow-minded."

It should be clarified that the coroner is not necessarily a physician. In fact, by law the coroner cannot conduct autopsies (in Dan's state). Instead, in order to preserve the integrity of the findings an independent autopsy must be performed. It is then up to the coroner to employ those findings in their report. It is in the respect that Dan says, "My job really is to bridge the investigations of the pathologist, police, and state's attorney. I serve as a point of interpretation, going each way, for all involved. For example, I am not a pathologist, I am simply an elected official, although I have enough experience working with pathologists to know how to interpret their results. And, having been a police officer and a state's attorney investigator, I know what it is they want from a pathologist, and how they go about making their cases. You see, I spent 10 years in charge of the city's homicide bureau, so I know how to investigate murders."

On the latter point it is important to understand that context is critical to a complete and successful understanding of someone's death. This means that not only crime scenes should be preserved, but you must have an understanding of the community, and the various agencies and departments which have an interest in the death. According to Dan, "After more than 28 years in law enforcement I know anybody that's anybody on a first name basis. And not just other police officers, but citizens of this community. While I have some authority, like the power of arrest and subpoena, it's who I know and what kind of relationship we have that I must rely on the get the job done." Consider the opposite as a case in point. Assume that a murder occurs in a part of the city about which you know absolutely nothing. It might be reasonable to assume that people in the neighborhood have some idea about the murder, but with no knowledge or contacts there how likely are you to get at the truth? Now assume that you are talking about neighborhoods which are strongly ethnic in character, including language and socio-economic class. With little or no knowledge of that neighborhood how likely is it that you will correctly interpret that death? The point is, what we informally refer to as 'context' can be essential to successful resolution of an investigation."

The preceding scenario becomes even more critical when there is a high frequency of cases. According to Dan, "In the past year we had 50 homicides and three years before that we had 92. Our average is more nearly 90 plus. That means a homicide every 3-4 days. With a staff including myself, a chief deputy, two secretaries, and ten lab personnel you can see for yourself how busy we are. Add to this an average of 1600 deaths per year, 500 of which are coroner cases. We are always doing some kind of investigation here." Coroner cases are those deaths which are medically unattended. "Our job in most of these cases is to eliminate the death as a homicide, suicide, or accident; to establish that it was a natural death. The problem is that knowing and proving may be two different things. This is where knowledge of the community is so important. Your best weapon is someone else's information."

Ultimately, the conclusion generated for any particular death is a function of teamwork and consensus. The coroner must coordinate the efforts of people who may, and are often likely, to have competing interests. Particularly in a murder investigation the coroner must balance medical, law enforcement, state's attorney, political and public interests. "Unfortunately," according to Dan, "things do not work the way they often seemed to on that television show, Quincey (a popular 70's and 80's television series about a west coast coroner). People always expect us to be able to pinpoint everything, like time of death. While we can estimate, we cannot pinpoint. This means that timing is most important. The sooner we are on the scene the better our chances are of being right. So, until we have finished with a crime scene I always make it a rule to have someone there protecting the evidence."

Today the process of investigation has become very technologically dependent. But in some very high profile cases (for example Jon Benet Ramsey, the British au paire, and O. J. Simpson), it has become very obvious that technology does not speak for itself, nor is it unambiguous. Data must still be interpreted. And, out of context is still out of context, which means that understandings will vary according to perception. It is the management of this which is the heart of the coroner's inquest. It is in the inquest where citizens are convinced of one interpretation or another.

Ultimately, the test of the coroner's work is acceptance by the public. Here we see another aspect of the role, public relations. Most would not see this, at least initially, as important to the job. But if the court of public opinion is consistently against you then you will not be long for the coroner's job. For this reason, according to Dan, "I have a policy that news releases and other public statements are only from myself or my deputy. It is too easy to be caught in real or perceived contradiction. Whenever you are out in front, where the public and media can see you easily, and your position is potentially high profile, you have to be very careful. Further, you have to be able to stand the heat, the stress. Otherwise, the truth will be compromised."

Dan suggests that there are specific aspects of the job which are often overlooked, but are still essential. One is the ability to read people. According to Dan, "I have a 'street' degree in psychology. I've learned through experience how to figure out others." A second is confidentiality. "You have to know how to keep your mouth shut. It is so easy to compromise an investigation by shooting your mouth off. Or, you can create all kinds of misleading impressions by speaking when you really don't have a conclusion. Those kinds of things can really get you into trouble in a political environment." A third aspect is respect. "You are dealing not just with a body, but a family, friends, a neighborhood, a church, or a community. You need to be sensitive to their sense of loss, their customs, and their needs. This is especially true of identification. On the one hand loved ones want to know the fate of a friend or family member. But at the same time they usually hope the John Doe in your morgue is not theirs." Finally, you need to be able to separate yourself from emotional involvement. "For example, you have to have a strong stomach. We see some really awful stuff, and some heart wrenching stuff. If you get too involved in the emotions of the situation there is no way you can do this job. You also need a means of relieving the death stress. And you have to be ready to go 24 hours. People can die at very inconvenient times."

Assuming you can hold up to the stresses of such work, what should you as students, and potential coroners, be doing to prepare? Dan has some interesting recommendations. While he himself does not have a college degree he says a college degree is "essential." Dan's education included special courses in police training, investigation science, various classes in law and forensic pathology. However, it is not essential to have a specific criminal justice or science background. The reason is that the job of the coroner is so much broader than the lab or the law. It is about ". . . coordinating the necessary resources to arrive at the truth." And this involves everything from management skills to cross cultural understanding, to public relations, to a general understanding of the law and its various agencies. For theses reasons Dan recommends ". . . a generalist degree, but one which includes casework in communities, psychology, sociology, and if possible, investigation services. It is essential to be well-rounded with excellent people skills. Finally, if at all possible, get experience such as an internship. It is in such experience that you can see if the coroner's work is for you."

8

STATE POLICE TROOPER

Caleb Manns is 30 years old and in his tenth year as a state police trooper. Knowing this may tend to narrow your conception of Caleb's work; however, this would produce a very skewed perspective. For in those 10 years Caleb has served as a trooper on patrol, in a K-9 unit, gang unit, conspiracy unit, and as a special agent. So far Caleb has had training in K-9, drug interdiction, covert operations, surveillance, conspiracy, motor carrier safety, and internal investigations, to name just some. The fact is, according to Caleb, "Crime and criminal law are always changing, consequently, you're never done with testing and training."

In high school Caleb actually had two different sounding, but related career aspirations. "On the one hand I thought about going into the ministry. It was important to me to believe in certain values and try to live up to them. I also saw the ministry as oriented to helping people. I could see myself in that role and wanted some way to develop that interest. On the other hand I think law enforcement has always been a part of me in one way or the other. I think that I always admired the uniform, what it stood for, the idea of being an officer, and the professional image which all of this projected. And, I saw officers as helpful to people. In this way it was somewhat like the ministry. Both careers have strong orientations to the service of others." During this time Caleb began talking with the local chief of police, asking his advice, and checking out various colleges and universities. He was also investigating options for pursuing the ministry.

The initial result of Caleb's deliberations was a decision to pursue the ministry, and in the fall of 1986, he enrolled in a church related college. While there, a graduate of that school came to campus on one occasion to speak. The speaker related that after graduation he had gone on and completed a bachelor's degree and eventually joined the state police. At the same time as this visit Caleb had been reconsidering just what it was he wanted to do. According to Caleb, "The visit was really pivotal for me. It gave me renewed focus, and I decided that I wanted to pursue some kind of degree in law enforcement." In the fall of 1987, Caleb transferred to another school where he could complete an AA degree, and search for a program where he could finish a degree in criminal justice.

In 1988 he found such a program, one ranked nationally among all such programs, and transferred there for his junior year. The program, a BS in Law Enforcement Administration was, according to

Caleb, ". . . especially strong in its faculty. We had faculty who had served in the FBI, local and state police departments, as state's attorneys, and in fire departments, among other agencies. I also joined the student's law enforcement organization, Lambda Alpha Epsilon. I was even president for a term. Through this organization we were able to bring in a lot of guests from different kinds of law enforcement agencies. The whole idea of this program was to get as close as we could to people in the field, see things from their point of view, and ask all the questions we could think of." Partly as a result of such programming Caleb decided in his first year there to go ahead and take the state police exam, ". . . just to see how I would do, and where I might fit in."

Somewhat, but not wholly to his surprise, Caleb did well on the exam. According to Caleb, "The exam seeks to assess your ability to process information quickly and accurately. You are tested on your perceptions, your honesty, integrity, and your general intelligence." Caleb actually did well enough to make the cut for the next stage of testing. This next stage included a number of other tests and procedures. He was given a psychological interview in which his personal history was explored and he was evaluated for emotional stability. He was given medical tests and was evaluated for physical fitness. He submitted to a general oral interview, and had a background check. Interestingly, Caleb was not evaluated on what he knew about criminal law, the use of weapons, or whether he was familiar with standard police procedures. According to Caleb, "It did not matter what my degree was. They were looking for your ability to be trained and your future capacity to be a state police officer."

During the interview process Caleb was asked about his education goals. "I told them that it was important for me to finish my degree, and I found that they were also interested in this. At that time a four year degree was not required, but beginning in 1999 it will be. They apparently wanted to hear this because in the fall of 1989, my senior year, I was offered a position as a state police cadet. This was the first step necessary to being admitted to the academy." The problem, of course, was the timing of the offer. Caleb still had credits to complete for his Bachelor's degree. If he were attending the Academy then this would obviously interfere with college. However, according to Caleb, "My faculty and the program were happy that I'd been offered a spot. While it was out of the ordinary, they were able to work out a series of independent studies so that I could finish my degree while employed with the state police." Caleb accepted the appointment and entered a 20 week academy. During this time a cadet's salary is figured at about $25,000 per year.

According to Caleb, "I really wish I had paid more attention to the basics while I was in high school and college. It really did not matter at all what my major was. They were going to train me the way they wanted me trained. What was necessary was that I was willing and able to learn what they were teaching. But the emphasis was on basic skills. For example, English and composition are useful for all the report writing you do, history is important so that you can understand the reason for the system of laws we have, math for something as simple as accident calculations, and sociology or psychology for insights into human behavior."

After graduation from the academy a cadet is a probationary trooper for the balance of the year. The salary rises to about $27,000 per year. During the probationary year the new trooper goes to work under the supervision of Field Training Officers (FTO); usually at least three different ones. Their purpose is to evaluate and critique the new trooper's work, particularly with the public. According to Caleb, "The initial emphasis is criminal law and the state's vehicle code. You are continually tested on your knowledge of the law. However, it is in the application of the law that you are really challenged. Coming out of the academy so any things seem so black and white. But you soon find out that the real world is never so clear. Black and white very quickly became all shades of gray. Now you must use discretion; it is a necessary skill. Because you are always working with people you are required to exercise judgment. One distinction you have to make is whether you make an arrest on the basis of the likely prosecution, or whether it is simply a matter of a broken law. You must have credibility with state's attorneys that an arrest you make will stick. It was the job of the FTO's to help us learn this distinction. Sometimes an FTO would step in and remind us of the need for discernment. Other times they would let us learn by our mistakes."

Two other critical lessons, hopefully driven home by the FTO's, is report writing and networking. According to Caleb, "You just have to be so clear and precise in your reports. You have to understand just how many people are likely to read what you've written. Included are other personnel in the state police, state's attorneys, judges, defense lawyers, maybe even appellate courts, and often the media. If each reader gets a different picture of what took place then your case is sunk. You are only as credible as your reports. And, if you hang too many people out to dry, such as state's attorneys, then your credibility will be shot."

The other lesson is working relationships. Actually, your written reports are one aspect of your working relationships. But in addition, there are a whole host of other law enforcement relationships which you must cultivate. Any investigation requires the cooperation of others, both within the agency and among agencies. For example, there are always overlapping districts. You must have an awareness of jurisdictions, where you are, and whose turf you are working. According to Caleb, "You must be especially careful not to step on anyone else's toes. A crime is committed within a sheriff's department's jurisdiction. But it may involve other possible crimes and criminals in other locations, or you may even be involved in a pursuit. If you just ride in like the Lone Ranger or John Wayne you will certainly not get the needed cooperation. As a new trooper this is often difficult to resist, but your FTO's must instruct you on this. Over time you will develop your own personal network of peers in law enforcement. You will eventually become quite dependent on this as you engage in routine investigations, and not so routine work such as surveillance, drug interdictions, or covert operations. If you can't trust your contacts and peers, then you simply cannot do the job. How else are you going to get background information, for example, from another state?"

Since becoming a trooper Caleb has trained for, and spent time in, a number of special state police units. This, according to Caleb, has kept his work always interesting, never dull. For two years Caleb was part of a K-9 unit. To this end he did three months of intensive training with a dog, followed by two days per month of additional training. According to Caleb, "Ultimately you have to trust your dog. Part of this trust is built by always being together." Some of the specific training included searching for missing people, including children and older people, tracking, school and vehicle searches, and training for aggression and attacking. One of the more noteworthy tasks of Caleb's K-9 work was the successful tracking of an escaped murderer from prison. At the end of two years the dog was retired to Caleb, and now is a part of his family.

For the next two years Caleb worked on a gang unit. "In gang work you really have to get into the mindset and culture of gangs. You have to figure out their patterns of communication. Typically this training occurred in urban areas. The problem is that many local agencies are not really prepared for gangs. Gangs can be quite mobile and therefore especially problematic. Our job took several tacs to the problem. We sometimes did gang suppression sweeps or worked covertly from vehicles. What we were trying to do was let the gangs know that they were being watched. If they believed this then they either cut down on their activity or sometimes left the area."

Subsequent to this Caleb was assigned to a criminal conspiracy unit. According to Caleb, "This work often centered around mid-level drug dealers. When a dealer was caught with drugs we would use them to work either direction toward the source or towards distribution, in order to more thoroughly interfere with the drug organization. Other kinds of conspiracy work involved investigations of bank records, property, credit history, college grades, and other paper trails. The idea is to see if assets and lifestyles actually match. If not then there may be more than meets the eye." Of course, law officers cannot investigate just anyone. There must be cause. This is where cooperation among local authorities is critical. Caleb is now a special agent, engaged in inter-agency investigations, and investigations of government personnel. Such investigations require an integration of skills. Caleb is presently continuing his training in this particular unit.

After 10 years on the force, Caleb has a number of suggestions for aspiring state police troopers. The first is to understand that being a trooper does not specify any one kind of law enforcement work. In fact, as Caleb's career illustrates, there is great diversity in such work. For this reason Caleb recommends a " . . . diverse education. Do not prepare narrowly. Remember, the academy will train you in ways the state police see fit. Furthermore, once you are a trooper you will always be in some stage of training. Do not ignore the basics. Especially, be able to write clearly and to the point. More and more, police officers need to be able to speak, whether it is community groups, classes, children's schools, or courtroom testimony. It is also the case that computer literacy is becoming more and more in demand. You must know how to turn them on and access relevant information. Most importantly is an appropriate orientation to the community. In order to do the job, law enforcement agencies require the assistance of the public. The kinds of relationships you have in the community is directly related to the success of your efforts."

Caleb now earns about $51,000 per year, with a raise due soon to about $55,000. Caleb feels he is being compensated well for his work. At the same time he believes he is contributing a vital and professional service to his community. He recently considered a move to the FBI but has recommitted himself to his work. "As long as I can continue to develop within the state police, every 2-3 years taking on a new challenge, then this is where my career will stay."

9

STATE PROBATION AND PAROLE BOARD

Val Michaels, aged 53, is now a regional administrator for the state parole Board with responsibility for planning and budgeting. But Val's position is more than a job. In fact, Val's work in this branch of criminal justice carries some aspect of the pioneer within it. According to Val, "In the 1960's I majored in sociology. It was certainly a time of major and sometimes radical change. As an African-American it was an exciting time. A time of hope and promise. Sociology was a natural fit for me. But it also revealed to me many aspects of society which were troubling. Quite frankly, minorities were significantly underrepresented in nearly all aspects of social policy. It was apparent to me that if minorities were to make any real progress then they had to be in positions of leadership where social policy was being defined." One such area was criminal justice. When asked why criminal justice, Val responded, "My grandmother actually served as a referee in juvenile court from the 1920's through the 1940's. And, she served in the juvenile probation office. Growing up, this is what I knew. In many ways, just like my major in sociology, it was natural for me to end up in this field."

After graduation Val took a while before settling into her career path. Initially she worked for the Tennessee Valley Authority, then returned home where she took a position as a juvenile probation officer; the same kind of work as her grandmother. However, she did not stay there long and eventually relocated to another city and sat out a year. Then in 1970 Val went to the state office of probation and parole looking for a position. But she was not hired due to a perceived lack of experience. Though, as would become clearly evident, Val had more than just experience, she had perspective and know-how as well. So, she went immediately to get the formal experience she was told she lacked. For two months she worked as a bond investigator, conducting various kinds of pre-trial investigations. According to Val, "I was just waiting until a probation officer's position became available." Such a position became available in 1971. Two years later Val became a unit manager.

Val's qualifications had become quite obvious and she was on a fast track to bigger challenges. In 1975 she entered a Master's program in corrections at a local university. In 1977 Val became involved with the American Correctional Association (ACA), and by 1978 was president of the state affiliate of the ACA. Other organizations with which Val associated included the National

Association of Blacks in Criminal Justice, the Association of Paroling Authorities International, and the American Probation and Parole Association. In addition to all these participations, Val was promoted to District Supervisor in 1978.

There were a number of advantages produced by all this activity, and Val's rapid rise in the state system. According to Val, "I was positioning myself so that I could influence the direction and future of probation and parole. As I said before, it was important for blacks to be in position to influence social policy. I was doing this through my associations. Among other things, I was organizing various conferences and workshops. This was still unusual for a black person. But it was giving me visibility and an opportunity to have a say in things. It also taught me about organizations and organizational skills. Throughout your career such skills can prove invaluable." This latter point was especially significant. According to Val, "In addition to visibility and policy, my work in the various associations benefited me in terms of personal networking. Your relationships to others are critical in terms of your ability to have access to information, power, or authority. Without such relationships you are essentially alone. Your network is not only a means of accessing a particular resource, but is also the means of influencing trends or movements within the profession. People all across the country were only a phone call away."

1984 saw a culmination of Val's career efforts. She was appointed by the governor to the State Parole Board. According to Val, "This was one of my career goals. It was important, for many reasons, to have reached this level. One, it validated my work in the profession. Two, it justified the faith that my peers and mentors in agency work had in me. These people have been so critical to any success I have had. Three, I could now serve as a mentor to others. While I might have already been doing this through work in the agencies, and within the professional associations, my new position gave me enhanced credibility. Four, I now had an additional platform for impacting public policy. And five, it was important that I, as a black person, could now serve as a role model for others."

The State Parole Board is a bipartisan entity appointed by the governor. As a quasi-political body the Board is to be comprised of two Democrats, and three Republicans or three Democrats and two Republicans. Its responsibility included oversight administration for approximately 1000 probation officers, in addition to some specific duties. These include holding parole hearings, deciding on inmate releases, as well as returning some probationers and parolees to prison, and general correctional strategy. While the Board is indeed a quasi-political body, Val " . . . was never politically involved. I was credentialed, but not politically savvy. All my contacts were in the profession, not in the parties." This would eventually create new challenges for Val.

After she had been appointed to the Board Val only then realized the political nature of the job. "This," according to Val, "was part of my naiveté about the position. In fact, the position I was appointed to fill was actually a Republican seat, and I am a Democrat. So, when I was first nominated I actually did not get the seat. However, just after that the state legislature expanded the Board from three to five members and I was appointed. At that time my appointment was for four years. In 1988 I was reappointed for an additional six years." In 1994 Val received the top American Correctional Association award; another highlight in a career which had run the gamut from entry level to top state post. However, the politics about which Val initially knew very little, eventually caught up with her. "In 1994, although I'd won the ACA award, I was not reappointed for another term. I was replaced by a white Republican male. It was, absolutely, a political appointment. And for the first time in 25 years, I felt that my credibility had been overwhelmed by politics. Now, four years later, I can say that I don't actually regret the process being political. But politics is the only reason I am not on the Board right now."

In the past few years the whole field of corrections, including probation and parole, has come under close public and media scrutiny. The political climate has tended to exacerbate the emotions people have about crime and punishment. For example, federal sentencing guidelines have restricted judicial flexibility and imposed longer, determinant sentencing. Programming and "luxuries" such as Pell Grants for college level education and exercise equipment, have been systematically withdrawn from our prisons. In political campaigns law and order are frequently touted, often including "Willie Horton-like" commercials criticizing the probation and parole policies of one or another candidate. The point is that corrections generally, and agencies specifically mandated to deal with criminals, are always subject to public and political winds. In this regard, Val believes that, "While the decisions of the Parole Board are not typically politically pressured, the Board nonetheless is always responding to society, to what is going on in the community. This means that certain trends in society will find their way into Board thinking, and ultimately Board decisions."

Sometimes social trends run head-on into practical reality. For example, the "lock them up and throw away the key" trend eventually encounters the ability of states to pay for enough prison space. When the cost per inmate begins to run at $25,000 - $30,000 per year, then the public begins to reconsider. In a number of states this has been addressed through "contract" prisons; that is, assigning inmates to private prison facilities and management companies. But then again, in those instances where contracting has gone awry, such as poor treatment of inmates, the public has typically called for investigations, or even termination of contracts. The volatility of the issues, according to Val, " . . . is a function of the fact that society is so motivated by fear. This makes for a very up and down pattern." However, the issues of crime and punishment will always be with us. And, as one trend reaches its limits, whether they are the limits of budget or the limits of conscience, then we typically see some kind of reversal. They key is to be well positioned in order to make a difference. This is what Val has done, and continues to do. But what can students, who are interested and concerned about such issues, do now? What are the career implications of Val's career?

According to Val, "While I said that probation and parole was part of my upbringing, I must say that my degree was not really career motivated. My idea of a career developed after I was on the job. I really credit certain people, who come along at various times in every career, as mentors. Actually I count three such mentors in my career. Their input was critical. Mentors do at least three things for you. One, they teach and advise you about the work at hand. They are people who can walk you through the tasks, problems, and issues of work. Perhaps more importantly, they introduce you around to others in the field or profession. This is the second impact of mentors. By doing so, mentors help you construct essential networks. Finally, mentors can be a career sounding-board. They can take your ideas and advise you as to what you should be considering regarding your career." But how do you get a mentor? In some instances it just seems to happen. But understanding their importance you can begin now, seeking them out. One excellent source is via internships while in college. Do not be timid. Ask questions and make it a point to be with others. Showing an interest in them will help produce an interest in you.

As far as degrees, Val says that if you are actually pursing a career in probation and parole, sociology and/or psychology are typically required. Bachelor's degrees are also required. In some settings bilingual and cross cultural skills are necessary. While not required in many places it is certainly on the horizon. Computer literacy is a must. Writing skills are critical. Officers are always writing reports. And as a member of the State Parole Board, Board members have to be able to articulate and defend decisions. This is obviously an issue of communications; those directed within, to correctional, probation, and parole officers, and those directed to the public and the politicians. How you present yourself and your ideas or positions is important to your success in doing so.

In conclusion, Val wants students to know that, "Being an officer in probation and parole can be a wonderful job for life, or an excellent job as a stepping stone to other career possibilities.

However, it is not generally the kind of career which is especially financially rewarding. Salaries range from $25,000- plus, based on experience, for first-time officers, to $60,000 annually for Parole Board members. What this means is that you must have motives other than money for this kind of work. The motive must be a belief in the value and potential of people to reclaim their lives, and become once again contributing members of society.

10

CIRCUIT COURT JUDGE

Judge Joel Kessinger has seen all sides of the criminal justice system in his nearly thirty-five years of service, "I've prosecuted felonies, and I've defended the accused. I've sentenced convicted murderers to death and I've sentenced a man convicted of reckless homicide to repeatedly put flowers on the grave of the person he killed." Now 61, Joel has been a judge since 1989. He was elected to the Circuit Judge position in 1996, and will hold that position until 2002. When asked if he will run for re-election, Joel says, "It all depends on whether I feel like it. Being a judge is an awesome job, and an equally awesome responsibility." Just how Joel came to this position is a story full of twists and turns, and a life dedicated to a philosophy of learning from your experiences and seizing your opportunities, whatever they may be.

Joel was an involved high school student; award winning football player and student body president. He was also a young man accustomed to work, spending seven summers in the steel mills. In 1956 he graduated from high school and spent the next two years at an all boys junior college in Kansas. "I was really following my big brother," says Joel. After two years Joel graduated with a degree in arts and sciences and transferred to a four year university near home in order to complete his education. "I was majoring in English with a minor in education and history. My goal was to be a high school teacher in English or history, and to coach football. But during my junior year I was talking with a neighbor, a lawyer, about various things, including my education and my plans for the future. One thing became apparent. Most of the teachers I knew were also working in the steel mills during the summer, just as I had been doing. Here I was working as hard as I could to get a degree, and I could still end up back in the mill in the summertime. This was a disappointing realization. At the suggestion of my lawyer friend I began thinking about law. It was late in the summer before my senior year, nearly too late to do anything much different. Besides , I had never even thought of law as a career. But my neighbor went to bat for me, and I did have good grades. The result was that I was admitted to two law schools for the coming year. Of course, I'd had no idea that there were programs for admission after the third year of undergraduate studies. For very basic reasons, housing in particular, I stayed where I was and enrolled in the law school. However, because of my ignorance of the possibilities, I failed to transfer my first year of law school credits back to an undergraduate program, thereby completing an undergraduate degree. So, while I have a law degree, and six years of higher education, have practiced law, and now am a judge, I do not actually have a college degree!"

The path to law and the judges role, however, was not yet to be so direct. In Joel's last year of law school five of his friends were planning on joining the FBI. "They thought that law degrees would give them an advantage in being selected. Since I lived locally and had a car, my friends asked me if I would take them to the Federal Building where they could make application. They, of course, were dressed for the day and otherwise prepared for the process. As luck would have it I found a parking space right in front of the building, and it even had time on the meter! I wasn't dressed at all for a test, let alone an interview, but my friends persuaded me to give it a try. So I did. I went with them, tested, and had a brief interview. At the end of the day, out of six of us who applied, I was the only one accepted!"

Later that year Joel received his appointment letter to the FBI. In August of 1962 he entered the FBI Academy, then split between Washington, D.C., and Quantico, Virginia. "My main motivation at that time was economic. Remember, I had changed course in college due to my disappointment with the economic prospects of a career in teaching. With the FBI, I was offered a salary of $12,000. In 1962 that was a salary greater than all other of my fellow graduates from law school. However, near the end of my training my younger brother was killed in a football game. My father had died years earlier and my mom was really in need of help. I decided that I would see if I could get an assignment somewhere in the vicinity so that I could be near and take care of my mom. I found that was not an easy thing to do, and I even had two personal meetings with the Director of the FBI, Hoover. But it didn't work out. So, I resigned from the FBI, returned home, and went into private law practice."

In 1964 Joel started down a career path which mixed politics and law enforcement for the next 25 years, until he was first appointed as a judge. In that year he was appointed as an Assistant State's Attorney. The State's Attorney's office is a political office with responsibility for prosecuting crime in a particular county, or in some cases a specific district (hence, the D.A.). According to Joel, "Well, I had the law degree, and had passed the Bar, and I also had that identity of being with the FBI. Together, with my background in the local community, it was a rather natural fit." The position was actually part-time, so Joel kept up with his regular law practice. But it did allow him to begin learning the in's and out's of local politics and law enforcement. "Actually," according to Joel, "my work was concentrated in the felony division. My agreement called for work on 12-15 felony cases per month. I didn't work according to time. If I finished those cases early then my time was free to pursue other things."

Because of the political nature of the state's attorney's office Joel was not guaranteed a job. According to Joel, "I am a Democrat and as long as there was a Democrat in office then I had work. When a Republican took office I was no longer with the State's Attorney's office. In the 25 years prior to being appointed judge, I was out of office, so to speak for eight years. During that time I worked my private practice. Among other things, I defended accused felons. This aspect certainly gave me a rather unique perspective on how the court system worked, and what influence the community or political environment might have on the judicial process." Also during this time Joel kept busy by serving for a while as local city attorney, professor of criminal law, and other duties of a general law practice.

By having such an array of law related positions Joel came to understand critical skills in law practice. One was, every person is unique, and the circumstances in which they are involved are also unique. Generalization, while at times useful, nonetheless gloss over important aspects of any case. Because of this you have to be willing to, and learn how, to dig beneath the surface of any case. It is important to develop an appropriate sense of context. It does matter what else is going on in a person's life. Those other things certainly do influence how and why a person behaves the way they do. Further, a good historical perspective helps you understand any movement in society, including crime. This is not the same thing as an apology for the way things were done in the past. It is, rather, a means of better understanding the changes which we are constantly experiencing. Such things always impact how we perceive and respond to crime. An example, according to Joel, is the role of families in juvenile crime. "Over time what I have observed is the diminished presence of parents in the lives of children involved in crime. First it was fathers. Either by work, war, or just stepping out of family life, fathers have noticeably been removed from the lives of their children. This has obvious consequences, not the least of which is a missing adult role model for young boys and girls. These children do not know how an adult male should behave because they rarely see one. The other problem in this regard is authority. Whatever else fathers do, they establish and administer authority within the family. The fact is, it does make a difference in court whether there is a father in the family. Now, the father's role is no more important than a mother's role. History demonstrates that fathers have been periodically been absent in the lives of their children. But mothers have been the constant. You may not have a father, but you always have a mother. At least mothers seemed more present or durable in the lives of children. The more recent phenomenon is that as fathers continue to disappear, mothers have also begun to disappear. At the very least mom is at work, and children are left to other role models while they grow. Now, this does not mean that a mother who works will produce children in trouble with the law. But it does mean that if a mother's absence enhances the tendency of some to stray into poor choices and behaviors, the absent moms will accentuate this problem, especially if the father is already gone. In some cases, we just let the TV raise our kids." According to Joel, "It is obvious in my court, when a young kid is charged with a serious crime, that most often, father and mother, have been absent in that boy's life."

A second major skill, according to Joel, is communication. "You are always having to deal with all kinds of people. You must not just know how to speak, but you must be able to understand. This latter point is often overlooked when the issue is communication. The range of people and roles with whom you are connected in this field is really enormous. You have to be able to talk and discuss matters with all kinds of serious offenders. There are also the friends and family of those accused of crimes. Then you have victims, and those who care about them. Surrounding each of these are lawyers, prosecutors and defense, judges, and media. You have to be able to read what people mean, not just what they say. And, you have to be careful with what you say. If it can be taken wrong, it will. Experience is really the only effective teacher in this case."

In 1989 a trial judge position opened in the circuit where Joel had served. At that level there are two kinds of judges, associate and circuit. Qualified candidates are typically appointed by other judges, to the associate level first. Associate judges serve for four years before reappointment. Generally associate judges do not hear felony cases, or cases where money damages exceed $25,000. However,

41

associate judges may be certified by the Supreme Court to hear such cases. Circuit judges, which do hear such cases, and cases with money damages over $25,000, are not appointed but elected on a partisan ballot. This means that they run for election associated with a party. If elected, they serve a six year term. Re-election in six years is based on a retain or not retain basis. The vote is non-partisan, and to be retained a judge must receive 60% votes to retain, out of all votes cast. In 1989 Joel's appointment was to an associate judge's position. In just a few months he was certified for circuit level work. Joel was also assigned to the criminal felony division. While judges do tend to rotate, for example among family or juvenile courts, Joel's expertise has focused his work primarily in the criminal felony division. In 1996 Joel ran for circuit judge and was elected. His term will expire in 2002, but as mentioned, he is not sure at present just what he will do then. The typical salary at Joel's level is now about $120,000 per year.

As a judge, according to Joel, the skills are essentially the same ones he had been exercising all along. But the responsibilities are, as Joel says, "awesome." However, the focus of attention given to any judges are decisions they render. This is the most obvious point of attention to what judges do. So, how does Joel make such decisions? According to Joel, "As with the jobs of prosecutor or defense attorney, take each case on its merits. Treat each case as a unique case. You are dealing with real people and real lives. In many instances you are dealing with true tragedy. And, no matter how much you try, you can never put all things back as they were before some act, or crime, changes it all. All you can hope to do is make progress from where you are. In the states you tend to have more discretion, or latitude in deciding a case or a sentence. In federal court judges tend to be much more restricted. My mandate is to seek a rehabilitative solution, if not already required by law to impose certain sentences. To this end I have to use all that is available to me to make such decisions. What I rely on is life experience. I've raised a family of six and I understand a few things about why people do what they do. But I have also had a wealth of other life experiences. There is no magic wand. You can only do what you think is best. It really comes down to what I think is best in the particular case at hand. There are some trends, but you must be careful to decide only on the merits of the case, not the trends. Nonetheless, if there is a trend, it is that I've seen a reluctance on the part of all sorts of people in society to accept that actions have consequences. They do have consequences. If there is a perspective that I have, it is that people in my court must understand that their actions produce consequences, and they must somehow deal with them. In some cases this means prison and punishment, in others it means rehabilitation, or something still more creative. But if I can get people to take responsibility for their actions, and themselves, then we have made progress in their lives."

In conclusion, Joel's career has had both a logic, and its share of chance. Joel had made choices based on economic need and decisions based on the potential for someone to change their lives. Joel is simply trying to get others to see their own lives more clearly and to make good choices on that basis. In effect, a life not unlike Joel's. While it would certainly be difficult to map out in advance, it was a life thoroughly lived and full of productive choices.

What choices, according to Joel, can students now begin making which will produce the kinds of results desired? "Actually," according to Joel, "students from all academic disciplines are welcome. You can come to law school from a variety of perspectives. And, I see this as positive for the

42

profession. We need broadminded people and clear-minded people in this position. In a classic sense, I'm talking about being well-read. But not all insight comes from class. It comes from life well-lived. Travel, work, take on new and challenging experiences. Each of these contribute to you in ways both tangible and intangible. Ultimately, they give you a wealth of perspective upon which you can make the best choices possible for yourself and others." When it comes right down to it, this is exactly what we ask a judge to do.

11

POLICE DEPARTMENT - CIVILIAN ADMINISTRATOR

Andy Lebard is 54 years old and has been a part of law enforcement for only the past 8 years. While this may seem rather late in life for someone to make such change, it is illustrative of the evolving nature of work and careers. Change must be assumed. In the case of Andy, however, change after nearly twenty years in city government to police administration is not an indication of somehow having missed earlier career opportunities. Rather, Andy is now on the cutting edge of developments in law enforcement administration. His title now is Police Administrative Services Commander, in other words, the civilian equivalent of the chief of Police. But before going on, how did Andy get to this significant level of responsibility in law enforcement?

Andy earned his BS degree in business administration in 1967 and took an entry level position in management. Andy served as the Director of Admissions and Personnel for a hospital. He also worked in accounting. According to Andy, "It was a job." This was not where he envisioned his future, it was more a function of necessity. He had graduated and " . . . it was time to work."

However, just working is not what Andy was about. Andy began an MA program in Education with a focus on institutional counseling. He envisioned doing such work in an industrial setting, perhaps in training or personnel. Towards this end Andy's thesis was based on the development of an attitude scale for labor unions. Andy earned his MA in 1970. Subsequently, Andy worked on a Ford Foundation project as a researcher. In the project he tested a concept of financing and training for low-income persons and education.

It should be noted that while Andy was making progress by earning degrees and having diverse work experiences, he was not yet settled on the concept of a career. His work so far had been intentionally temporary as he pursued graduate studies. But this should not be construed as necessarily problematic. Andy was exploring and defining his interests. And this process continued as Andy decided to pursue his education at another institution. According to Andy, "I was thinking about studying more in the area of higher education with a focus on student personnel; maybe pursing a

Ph.D."

While enrolled in graduate studies focused on higher education Andy took a staff position at the university in student development. In part because of this work Andy began to refocus his interests. According to Andy, "I became somewhat disinterested in higher education, but I really enjoyed managing people and getting things done. I also found that research, not just pure management, was something that I liked." The result was a master's degree, awarded in 1973, in City Management and Public Administration. Within this degree was an emphasis in political science.

Upon graduation Andy spent about six months in a city management internship on the west coast. The experience, according to Andy, cemented his interests in city management and he began to interview for jobs with a desire to stay on the west coast. This he was able to do when he accepted a position as Budget Research Officer for a suburban community within a major metropolitan area. According to Andy, "It was a management position with a small staff and a significant amount of power and responsibility for a budget ranging up to $70 million." Among other important factors was a working knowledge of the police department budget and related matters.

Perhaps the most important "related matter" was the leading edge of a movement which could eventually impact all law enforcement agencies. This movement is generally referred to as "civilianization." According to Andy, in the city where he worked a new police chief came on board in 1986 and brought with him a desire to civilianize certain jobs within the department. What this means is that civilians, rather that sworn officers, began taking over duties within the police department which did not require the specialized training typically invested in a sworn officer. This would include jobs such as animal control, records management, training, planning, research and personnel. Civilianization does not occur where there is an issue of safety or the need for arrest powers in the job. For these a sworn officer is required.

The point of civilianization is essentially budgetary. First, communities may spend well over $100,000 in order to put a sworn officer in the field. These additional dollars are spent to pay, insure, train, and retire that officer. From a budgetary perspective it does not make much sense to invest so much in a person who will simply sit behind a desk, essentially not making use of his training, or engage in hazardous or arrest situations. Rather, communities are hiring persons trained in special areas, such as management information systems, crime scene investigations (i.e., dusting for fingerprints), etc. By doing so communities can hire specialists at much less cost than a sworn officer.

According to Andy, the new police chief saw civilianization as a potential trend for the future. In 1989 the process began with the buying-out of some long term police officers with early retirements benefits. These officers were replaced with various specialists, not other sworn officers. Furthermore, sworn officers were more and more assigned solely to duties commensurate with their training. Because of the financial implications of such change Andy, in his role as city budget research officer, both understood and was involved in the changes. Soon Andy was approached by the chief of police to make a switch from city management to the police department. In 1990 Andy made the change. He did so for a variety of reasons. According to Andy, "I wanted a change from seventeen years as budget director. I wanted something different. Besides, it was a challenge. I saw this as an opportunity and I took advantage."

While there is definitely a budget motive for civilianization Andy believes his general management and people skills have been important in implementation of this new program. According to Andy, "This change is really difficult. And, it has been quite slow." While seven sworn officers were initially bought out, this does not mean that the civilian replacements have necessarily functioned smoothly within what is now a hybrid organization. With any such change, the first thing produced is resistance. In this case, by initially replacing supervisory personnel an immediate effect was to reduce the number of promotion slots for sworn officers. There has also been union opposition. According to Andy, "Given that I was already known and had some level of influence and respect within city government, has eased, somewhat, my efforts." In fact, he has found his management skills to be quite transferable. Specifically, according to Andy, "I actually spend a good deal of my time resolving people's problems. And I have to do this with all kinds of people in all kinds of situations."

As already mentioned, civilianization is a developing trend. How it happens, according to Andy, is unique to each department's experience. For example, Andy is the only civilian among 32 area divisional commanders. The issues are not simply internal to this department, but external as well in inter-departmental relations. While at the leading edge of the trend, it certainly seems the case that civilianization is happening. For example, significant strides have already been made in privatization in corrections; i.e., private jails. Regionalization is a corollary development. Rather than each department having all possible services in-house, some highly specialized services are shared, or rotated, to the department in need. Examples include dispatching, crime labs, and major case squads. The lesson here is, law enforcement work is changing. So, how can students prepare for a career in criminal justice?

First of all, according to Andy, there are a variety of futures; not just single tracks. Through civilianization people can come into law enforcement from a variety of angles. Andy, himself, is a good example. His background included degrees in business, education, and city management. He had worked in hospitals, research projects, and development for city administration. Now, as a Police Administration Services Commander he earns between $95 and $100 thousand per year. It is apparent that Andy's varied background is an asset, not a liability to modern law enforcement. Andy's advice to students is to not specialize in any narrow field. Andy knows of what he is speaking given that he has responsibility for hiring in the department. When looking at applicants Andy says, "I always look for a college degree first. The degree can be in any area. What is important is that you have a degree in something. The degree moves you to the top of the pile. The degree indicates a variety of personal traits such as persistence, determination, organization and potential, among others." While some degrees may be specifically helpful, such as a chemistry degree for work in a crime lab, it does not mean that you cannot work in a crime lab without such a degree. According to Andy, "There is so much training available to professionals within the criminal justice system that a wide variety of skills can be learned. What is required is an interest and an aptitude to learn." For example, the technological revolution now requires computer literacy for people who never thought it could be required of them. Many squad cars now carry laptops connected via cellular communications to central departmental computers. It is not required that a veteran officer already know how to employ this technology. What is required is that he/she is willing and able to learn. As a student contemplating a future in criminal justice it is critical that you assume your future will bring similar needs for change and acquisition of new skills and perspectives.

12

FORENSIC ANTHROPOLOGY

Phil Strahl has one of the most unique positions in law enforcement. His career had been with the state police and he now has the rank of captain, which is primarily an administrative post. What makes him unique is the fact that he is a forensic anthropologist. It is his job to take bodies, too decomposed to identify by normal means, and provide a lead as to who that person was. In many cases all he has is a skeleton, or a part of one, from which to make an identification. So specialized is this work that, according to Phil, there may be only about fifteen full-time forensic anthropologists nationwide. The rest are part time only, with assignments in universities and research institutes. So, how does one get in to such a line of work?

After graduating from high school in 1967 Phil entered the Navy. In 1972 he was discharged and working at a gas station in a small town which used to have a state police sub post. According to Phil, "Many of the troopers got their cars serviced at the station where I worked, and I worked on their cars. I eventually came across and old high school friend who was with the state police and attending the state police academy. We talked about the possibilities and it sounded good to me, so I decided to apply at the sub post." The result was that Phil decided to attend community college for the next two years part-time generally in the field of law enforcement. According to Phil, "One professor, a former sheriff, was very charismatic and created quite a following among students. However, the classes I took were not at all helpful when I went into the academy. They were not particularly advanced or relevant."

In 1975 Phil attended the State Police Academy for 22 weeks. According to Phil, "It was worse than boot camp. Interestingly, it was one of the first classes of state troopers thoroughly impacted by affirmative action. The entering class was approximately 50% women and minorities, while the other 50% was generally white and armed forces veterans like myself." Phil believes that there have been both benefits and challenges brought on by affirmative action. It has brought needed diversity to law enforcement which has had the effect of broadening vision. The challenge is how to best deal with standards and qualifications in order to produce the best force possible. This does include the need for broader vision and, cultural literacy and skills.

After graduating from the Academy Phil took his first "uniformed" assignment working the toll roads of a major metropolitan area. After a year he transferred in 1976, to another post where he served as what we generally think of as a state trooper patrolling highways. While in this second posting Phil again attended a local community college. "I was able to make use of my VA benefits. I took mostly electives in criminal justice, law enforcement administration and a lot of sociology." For four years Phil stayed at this post and continued taking courses as time and schedule permitted. According to Phil, "What happened was that I eventually became motivated to complete a Bachelor's degree . It was not absolutely necessary to what I was doing. It was more personally important. Ever since the third grade I had wanted to be an archeologist. In 1980 I was transferred again, so this time I enrolled in a four year degree program."

In 1986 Phil graduated. But he did so while still a full time trooper on road patrol nearly all this time. Discipline, determination and persistence were clearly evident in this degree odyssey which spanned fourteen years. Even then his final credits required some gymnastics in order to finish. "I had to take six hours of independent study due to some bad academic advice." Phil eventually ended up with a degree in anthropology with an emphasis in archeology. He also earned a minor in earth science. "I really did not intend to get a job with this degree. It was just interesting to me, as I already said. It was personally important to finish. I didn't finish because of my job."

While pursuing his education Phil began to make some lateral moves within the state police. Within any job or career lateral moves are those steps you take into a part of the career field which is beyond your immediate responsibility or expertise. Students should understand that this is a reality of career development, and they should prepare themselves to do so. In 1982 Phil joined the state police division of forensic services as a crime scene technician. Here he began to make some connections between his scientific skills and the needs in law enforcement. In 1985 Phil ". . . dug up a skeleton in a yard. I did it as an anthropologist and managed to impress the state police. As a result, they offered to send me to a major forensic anthropology school with instruction by Clyde Snow, a leading expert in the field, and the Smithsonian Institute." It was here that Phil learned, in more detail, the work of forensic anthropology and how it fit into the overall picture of law enforcement. According to Phil, "You should understand that my move into this field, much like my decision to apply back in 1972, was not part of a well defined plan. I actually rather drifted into this kind of work. I was at the right place at the right time." However, this should not be construed as simply accidental. Remember, there was 14 years of part-time education including classes in colleges and the police academy. Discipline, determination, and persistence, along with personal motivation to complete a degree, helped create the opportunities into which Phil suggests he "drifted."

Currently, Phil is a leading forensic anthropologist in the region with significant connections nationally. In his state he is the person the state police comes to for any such work. According to Phil, "Whenever there is a body in need of my kind of work the state police calls, any time of the day or night, and sends a plane to take care of me, and I just do my job. I also coordinate with certain other cities for forensic work which they cannot provide themselves. You see, there are only about 15 full-time working anthropologists within the American Academy of Forensic Sciences."

Because most bodies are identifiable by other means an anthropologist is not always called on a case. But, according to Phil, "When you need an anthropologist you really need one." In 1995, for example, Phil was called in on 39 cases. But only 19 were actual cases. Many times when a skeleton is discovered it turns out to be animal or prehistoric bones. Of those 19 actual cases 16 were away from the office. The national average is 5 - 10 per year.

Because his specific service is not needed daily Phil has had two other parallel career paths. On the one hand his work has caught the attention of other states, departments and research institutions. He has lectured in local universities and has been offered an opportunity to pursue advanced graduate studies. So far he has not chosen that route due to his years on the force and desire to continue doing the work he does. He attends coroner conferences, advising them of the services and potential of forensic anthropology. He has found that many do not know of his services. Phil has done some free-lance work for other states, including some in facial reconstruction. And, Phil has had overload cases from the Smithsonian Institute, and an open invitation to return there and do research.

His other career track had been as a state police administrator. He presently holds the rank of Master Sergeant. His work in this capacity is largely administrative. "I am responsible for three troopers and two civilian investigators. We have three death investigations each week. That is the highest rate per capita in the state. Such volume keeps us quite busy and my job is to see to it that we keep on top of the workload. The fact is, troopers are trained in forensic methods, and in combination with our excellent lab facilities, we do solve a lot of crimes. The state has made commitment to us, and we are productive. It is my opinion that we have some of the best crime scene investigators in the country and some of the best equipment. We are prepared to solve crimes, and we do."

In addition to the state police responsibilities Phil and his staff work hand in hand with a variety of other departments. Already mentioned were coroners, but Phil's staff also works with local police and sheriff's departments as well as state's attorneys. At times he simply writes reports and at other times he testifies. "Unless we are able to coordinate our efforts then very little gets done. You do have to be careful, however, due to issues of turf or territory and the reputation of the state police. If you ride roughshod over people you won't be called in, or at least not very early in the process and cases can go unsolved." It must be remembered that not all persons in the law enforcement chain are specifically trained in techniques critical to solving cases. The sheriff, coroner, and state's attorney are elected officials, and probably do have some level of political interest in cases. According to Phil, "People skills are simply necessary."

Regarding students' career plans Phil has some interesting information and advice. As a Captain he earns about $76,000 per year. Some of his staff may earn more because they have an opportunity for overtime whereas he does not. At 49 years of age, Phil has begun to think about retirement. At 30 years of service he can retire with 70% of full pay. He must retire by age 60 according to regulations. Regarding a future in law enforcement Phil advises students to, " Look around and investigate the possibilities." Education is valuable and specific skills are an asset. Degrees in the sciences, for example, facilitate a career in crime scene investigations. However, Phil reminds, all potential state police officers must be prepared to advance through the academy. Success there is measured by general intelligence, motivation, determination and persistence. Any area of study is applicable. Presently the academy convenes only periodically, relative to law enforcement need, and money for funding. Today, someone admitted to the academy will be paid at the rate of $34,000 per year. Upon graduation a Trooper will earn $35,000 per year plus annual raises of 5%.

Ultimately, future law enforcement officers--state trooper or otherwise--must be committed to the objectives of the force. Solving crime, and thereby protecting the public from future crime must be the overriding goal. If this is your personal mission, as Phil has demonstrated and said, ". . . there can be a real future for you in law enforcement."

13

CORRECTIONAL EDUCATOR

Catherine Starek is currently a Supervisor of Education for the Federal Bureau of Prisons. Her primary responsibility is supervision for all educational and recreational programming at a Federal Correctional Institution (FCI) in the Midwest. Working in a medium security prison with nearly 1,000 inmates is a job which gives more than just a few people pause. According to Catherine, "Most people wonder how any woman can work in that environment. And, it wasn't that long ago that women ran into real barriers to this kind of work. In fact, when I was hired for my first job with the Federal Bureau of Prisons I was fired before I even worked a day. However, I should explain. In 1990, I applied for a job as a teacher at Leavenworth Penitentiary. They needed someone with a specialty in reading and I had that. I had the other necessary credentials and they had the need, so I was hired. For some reason the people there did not initially clue in on the fact that I was a woman. But before I could report someone did, and I was called and told basically that because I was a woman I couldn't be hired. It wasn't exactly policy, but it was the way they did things there. Well, I was called back the next day and told that I did have a job, but it was in the camp, not the penitentiary. My guess is someone said that they could easily have a lawsuit on their hands if I chose, so they created a position at the camp for me."

With such an introduction you might think that Catherine would just as soon move on to something else. But nine years later Catherine is still with the Bureau, has been promoted, and is actively exploring her options for advancement within the system. "In 11 more years I can retire, at age 51 with 20 years of experience." The lesson is Catherine's career is captured in her orientation to the job as much as it is a reflection of a particular gift or talent. But I am getting ahead of the story . I will return now to the beginning.

Catherine graduated from high school and entered college in 1976. Her interest and major was pre-law. For personal reasons Catherine's progress towards law school was interrupted. She eventually resumed school and graduated in 1981 with a BS in education, a special emphasis in communication, and a minor in political science. Subsequently she entered a master's program in organizational communications, though she has not yet completed that degree. By 1983, Catherine was making use of her degree and was teaching speech and English in high school. During this time, Catherine found that balancing all the demands of family and work were steadily increasing. According to Catherine,

"When you teach in public school you find your time is consumed by all kinds of things both inside and outside of the classroom, whether it is club sponsorship, sports, attending events, or just working after hours to do your job. After three years, I decided to quit teaching to be a stay-at-home wife and mother."

Unfortunately, or fortunately as her life developed, Catherine's teaching certificate in Kansas lapsed. The certificate has to be maintained by continuing coursework, which is required for teaching in that state. By 1990, another personal circumstance, this time a divorce, created an immediate need for employment. Because her certificate had lapsed a return to teaching, at least immediately, was out of the question. It was the case, however, that Catherine lived in eastern Kansas where there is a concentration of prisons. These included the Federal Penitentiary at Leavenworth, both men's and women's state facilities, and the military prison at Fort Leavenworth. Being in education, Catherine knew of teaching opportunities in prisons. When she checked with the state facilities she found that, like public schools, she needed a current certificate. But when she inquired of the federal system she found that a certificate was not required, just the degree. The decision was made for her. She applied and was eventually hired for work in the camp in 1990. The camp is a minimum security support system for the penitentiary; usually without walls or fences.

For the next four years Catherine worked as a teacher in the camp. She was then promoted in 1994, to Acting Assistant Supervisor of Education for the penitentiary. After 14 months she was temporarily promoted to Supervisor for the next six months. During these years, Catherine notes, "I learned a lot about the Bureau, particularly from my fellow workers." Among those workers were an increasing number of women. According to Catherine, "In my first two years at Leavenworth women began to be hired for maximum security jobs. This included our first female correctional officer and the first female lieutenant. Now the job opportunities for women are booming." There are a number of reasons which might explain this change, but Catherine has some specific ideas. "Women are an important and natural part of society. Whatever else a prison is, it is a society, though small in scale. Among the qualities which women bring is a calming effect on inmates and staff. An all male environment is not natural in society, and has the potential for exaggerating any problem. I have found that most inmates are actually respectful of me and other women. Based on what I know, many of them are also respectful of their mothers. This may explain our calming effect. Occasionally you'll encounter inmates who lack respect for you. These people are dealt with by both the system of the prison, as well as by fellow inmates. Other qualities which women seem to bring include personal organization and an attention to detail. Both of these are critical to how we operate."

In 1996, Catherine took a promotional transfer to a medium security facility which is her present job; Supervisor of Education. According to Catherine, "My job is much like that of a school principal. I have responsibility for both inmate educational and recreational programming." To do the job for an inmate population of nearly 1,000 Catherine has 19 full-time staff and 4 contract staff. Of the full-time staff, 12 are in education and 7 in recreation. Inmates work on earning their GED's, as well as a limited array of other self-improvement programs. In recent years federal legislation has sought to make prison "tougher" on criminals. One result has been the elimination of recreational programming such as weights, some movies, and musical instruments. In education such legislation terminated the availability of PELL grants to help inmates pay for college courses. While Catherine understands the intent of such legislation, she does not always agree with it. "At Leavenworth I had inmates thoroughly occupied in classes, taking notes, reading, and developing their minds. Some even completed college degrees. When their sentences were up they had something to show for their time. When you lose your tools it is obviously more difficult to occupy them, to keep them busy. You see, we have had a shift in the kind of inmate we are now receiving. In the past, we would have someone like a bank robber, someone generally older and with variable sentencing. If they made progress they could get out sooner. Now we have a preponderance of drug-related criminals, often in their 20's or early 30's. Because of new sentencing guidelines they may be with us for 30 to 40 years. Keeping them busy, or at least occupied is usually important for their own safety, our safety as staff, and the safety of the public, especially local communities."

Among other responsibilities Catherine is primarily an administrator. She manages budgets of approximately $190 thousand in education and $45 thousand in recreation. She hires new staff and administers interns, develops work schedules, oversees staff discipline, hears staff concerns and problems, monitors and arranges for staff training and professional development (staff must have 16 hours of professional development per year), implements new programming, serves as a liaison to other departments, and handles inmate concerns. These are just a few of her primary job responsibilities. Catherine also serves in what is called, a collateral duty, jobs which transcend the immediate job descriptions and may impact any part of the institution. At present she is the prison's Hostage Negotiation Team Leader. Obviously this is a function required for prison disturbances. But it highlights an important part of prison work. You always rely on your fellow correctional workers doing their job, so that you can do yours. Ultimately, your life may depend on such interdependence. Other collateral duties can include, Special Operations Response Team, Disturbance Control, Firearms Instructor, Command Center Recorder, and Annual Training. In Annual Training staff can partake in institutional familiarization, CPR, self defense, forensics, and foreign language study. According to Catherine, "You need to understand that all prison employees are first and foremost federal correctional workers. As such we have all had the same three week Law Enforcement Training Program in which we learn self defense, firearm technique, and do classroom study in corrections."

The preceding account, though by no means exhaustive, gives us a glimpse of the range of duties and issues Catherine addresses daily. She obviously requires, besides energy, a wide array of skills and personal qualities and characteristics. These can all be developed, but at the outset one must understand that these skills are needed and are important. The first needed quality mentioned by Catherine is the ability to communicate unambiguously. According to Catherine, "You must have initiative and be proactive regarding the gathering and dissemination of information within the prison. You simply cannot make assumptions, you must meet issues and problems head on. Be an active listener with both inmates and staff. Actually, you are constantly gathering intelligence on all people in the prison, both inmate and staff alike."

Second, you must have a high degree of personal and structural organization. "Remember, the FCI is part of the government, and government is a bureaucracy. If you are sloppy in the details you will produce more problems than you can solve. There is also an immense amount of planning. The reason is that anything you desire to do affects so many other departments, staff and inmate alike. Therefore, you must have an array of other departmental contacts, and work those contacts, in order that you may coordinate your efforts."

Third, according to Catherine, "You must be both emotionally and mentally strong. If you have any personal problems or matters such as low self-esteem, be sure to understand that the inmates will find this out and use it to compromise you at some time." On this point Catherine noted that, "Before I ever came to this FCI, the inmate networks had already passed along a complete 'understanding' of who I was. This perception existed here before I even got here."

Fourth, professionalism is paramount. "You must stay in your role. This doesn't mean that you cannot or should not attempt to empathize. However, if you are less than professional in every regard, rest assured that the inmates will discover something." Specifically, according to Catherine, "You must establish ground rules, build a solid reputation, and then be sure to follow through with whatever you say." On this latter point, Catherine admonishes, "Be consistent! In many aspects working with inmates is just like raising children. Many times you have to say no. If you must, then do so clearly and back it up. Because of this you will always upset someone. However, you cannot take their outbursts or hate personally. You need to separate out the roles. Ultimately, in this way you produce respect. To get this you need to exercise personal character. Remember, each and every day you will be tested, both socially, as in your position, and personally."

Aside from these qualities Catherine suggests there are some skills you should consider acquiring if you seek a future in corrections. "You must learn to adapt to change. Change is an inevitable part of correctional work. Related is an ability to be with and work with all kinds of people. Basically, people skills are your primary asset." In other words, you must acquire basic social science understandings of others, and then act on them productively. Catherine also suggests, "Stay healthy and be in good physical condition. It is not always necessary to the job, but it is necessary to your prison image. If you abuse yourself or are out of control (poor habits) then you'll not get the respect you need. On the occasion of a prison disturbance, you must be able to support your peers. And, you want you peers to support you."

Regarding education Catherine believes, "It is not so much the specific degree you earn, as it is the fact that you have earned one." Think back to some class for which you had to do a major project. What did you learn? Can you remember the paper? Maybe. But more important than the paper topic, is the fact that you were able to organize your time and resources to do the job. This is what your degree ultimately signals.

Finally, Catherine wants you to know that, "Everyday is new and exciting in one way or another. It is definitely not boring. It is a constant challenge, even when it may be aggravating." The possibilities are nearly endless. It is an excellent career which contributes much to you as a person. It is also a financially sound career. As a GS12, a government job classification level, she now earns approximately $52,000 per year. Starting salary at the GS7 level is now about $30,000. "You are well paid for a challenging career. One which, as I have already said, is booming for women."

14

CRIME SCENE INVESTIGATOR

Larry Donaldson and Less Stanton are crime scene investigators. They hold a rather unique combination of roles in that they are civilians who can carry a badge, a gun, and have the power to arrest. They have served as sworn officers, for local police departments, but now they are attached to a state police post, and work crime investigations in conjunction with all kinds of law enforcement agencies. While similar in some respects, their stories will be presented separately.

Larry has been investigating crime scenes since 1978. He estimates that altogether he has worked approximately 500 homicides. Besides a 40 hour crime scene investigation school, Larry has over 780 additional hours of training and is internationally certified as a senior crime scene analyst. His training has included analyses of hair, carpet and other fibers, blood splatter investigation, fingerprinting (basic, advanced, and processing), photography, pathology and medical examination, and profiling. According to Larry, "Training is simply a part of what you have to do in order to be successful in this business. If you think you are ready to investigate a crime just because you have been to the academy, then think again. Once you start thinking that you know enough you are then in trouble. You are in this job to solve crimes, and you need every tool available to do so. This is why I re-certify every two years."

Larry's path to such a career is a function of both education and experience, both being important mentors of his craft. Out of high school Larry entered college during the Vietnam War. Subsequently, he was drafted and eventually assigned to the military police. Upon his discharge he took a position, in 1972, as a local police officer. Five years later, 1977, he transferred to a second department where he worked for he next 10 years. While in that department Larry, in 1978, studied for and became a crime scene technician. Still on patrol Larry responded to all cases. As his training progressed Larry became a major crime scene technician and later held the position of supervisor. In 1987, Larry transferred to a special program for crime scene investigation with the state police. Since then Larry has been in his present assignment. Today a person in Larry's position would be required to have a bachelor's degree, though the state police requirement is still an associate's degree (Some states have already moved to required the bachelor's degree for their state police recruits. The state where Larry works will soon be requiring the bachelor's degree as well). However, Larry earned his degrees after he began his career in law enforcement. Larry now has two associate's degrees, one in criminal justice and the second, an associate of science. He has taken hours towards a bachelor's degree, but has not yet completed it. Nevertheless, as was indicated earlier, Larry has not been thin on education, given over 780 hours of crime scene training.

According to Larry, "While I don't have the four-year degree, I have certainly valued and pursued education throughout my career. If given the opportunity I would probably have stayed in school and complete a bachelor's degree before working full-time in law enforcement. But, I have had certain opportunities to see the immediate relevance of my education as I have had to apply it directly to my work." Actually Larry believes in a broad educational background as the best preparation for what he does. According to Larry, "Sociology and psychology were really very important to the development of my perspective. In such courses you begin to understand the fact of preconceived notions and prejudices. The problem is most people don't even know they have such points of view. And, they also have no idea how limiting prejudices can be. The fact is, in my line of work you have to deal with all kinds of people. You investigate and interview people from all economic classes, and people from all ethnic and minority groups. The thing you have to remember is, no matter the person, or their position in society, when they are the victim of a crime, like a homicide, that they are in fact people. The families of a homicide victim hurt just as much regardless of their skin color or class. The courses I took which forced me to think about such things ultimately broadened my mind. In my opinion this is essential. In addition, you will have to find some way to work with all kinds of people while you are in an investigation. Some of these will be people you interview, while others are part of the larger neighborhoods or communities in which your investigation is taking place. If you are broad-minded enough you can begin to see things from their point of view, and perhaps, to even think as they think about certain things. I can't tell you just how important this is."

Related to this is a trend Larry sees in investigation skills. "Society is becoming very diverse, more so than black and white, or city and town. It is now becoming more important to understand culture and languages. If you are dealing with people where their first language is not English, then it is so easy to get off track or misunderstand. You need to realize what it is like and means to be a foreigner or a recent immigrant. So I see a coming need for multilingual and culturally aware officers."

There are other ways in which such coursework is also important. "One frequent skill we use is interviewing. You have to be able to successfully communicate, with anybody. And, you need to know, if for some reason, you can't do the job. On occasion you are better off having someone else come in and conduct the interview. Among those you interview are people who are witnesses to a crime, victims of a crime, and suspects of a crime. You have to pay attention not only to what people say, but what they don't say. And how they conduct themselves. Many times it is the nonverbal cues, which we all give off, that really puts you on to critical information. You have to both listen and observe. One of the very simple things you are trying to find out is whether the subject you're interviewing is telling the truth or a lie. Over all of this, is the fact that victims, and victims' families, or just the families in the case of a homicide, are usually very emotional. Crimes, especially homicides and other crimes of violence like rape, are damaging to all related people. They will be grieving in the case of death, as well as angry and/or frightened. Some people will hide facts so they can take the law into their own hands and take revenge on whomever they believe is responsible. The issue here is that you must be always aware of the people and the circumstances so that you can make progress towards the truth."

On the other side of the classroom, Larry recommends a broad familiarity with the sciences. In his work he has frequently had to do preliminary examinations of bodies. He has to decide what is necessary to collect as evidence, and he needs to know how to go about doing that. He must be able to collect evidence without destroying it. "I have to have a basic understanding of chemistry, physics, anatomy, and math. I am always identifying drugs, taking samples, and making calculations. You need to know which evidence needs to be collected quickly because it may deteriorate. You need to understand the threat of blood-born pathogens. And, you have to have a strong stomach. Homicides can really be nasty scenes. Beyond that I have stood in on autopsies in order to make sure that specific pieces of evidence were collected. You have to know what you need, what you are talking about, and what questions need to be asked. This is why part of my training has taken place in medical schools. This attention to details will not only help you solve the case at hand, but maybe even other cases. In one instance the collection and identification of one fingerprint in a crime scene, in turn led to the solving of 40 other cases."

Finally, according to Larry, it is important to understand the value of teamwork. "You simply cannot do this job without the help of others. Your people skills are necessary for working with victims and suspects, but it is equally necessary for work within field of law enforcement. In fact, the secret of successful law enforcement is contacts. For example, I keep class rosters from my various training schools. This way I can call on all sorts of people for advice, expertise, ideas, or just a connection to someone else. Just plain, sterile information won't get it. You need perspective. On this point, another category for contacts is the local police and sheriff's offices. Plus, you have to be careful with jurisdiction. It's like turf. You have to be able to call on someone you know, or be able to make acquaintances rather quickly. If you are seen to be taking over, you'll often get shut out or you could make things worse."

Les is a contemporary of Larry's, but has come to law enforcement by another route. In fact, according to Les, "I really didn't seem destined for any specific career early on. One way of looking at it is that sometimes certain events carry you into a career, rather than you making a specific and clear decision to pursue one. I'd say that it is how it was with me to a degree." Les grew up in what he termed, a "White ghetto. Pimps, thugs, and average Joe's were my role models." In the late 60's Les was drafted, went to Vietnam, and survived it to return. Upon returning, and with no clear idea of where he was heading, Les went to work in a steel mill and part-time in a store. He really had no plans, and a career, as such, was not part of his thinking.

Among other things Les subbed occasionally at a bar, the owner of which rented an apartment to him. As Les tells the story, "By one or two in the morning there was a city curfew and there was always some difficulty getting the last guys out of the bar. In particular, there were these fellows we called Night Riders. They were actually night shift deputies, who were not afraid to knock heads. Anyway, one old Night Rider gave me a hard time about 'last call,' and we had 'words.' About a week later I was out late and my car broke down, so I had to walk home. Some of these Night Riders pulled up and harassed me. We had some more 'words,' and I'm sure I showed a lot of attitude, but they went ahead and gave me a ride home! One was the same old Night Rider who'd given me a hard time before about closing the bar. But this time he just talked with me. While talking I told him about my job situation, and the fact that I really had no plans. Then he asked me if I wouldn't be interested in law enforcement. He said, at the very least, use the GI Bill to go to college. That really was good advice."

"So, I went to the local community college and enrolled in their night school. And the late classes were law enforcement! The courses were generally easy, and a lot of common sense." After some time Les decided to make application to several local police departments as well as the state police. He didn't make the state police class for the academy, but was hired by a local department. A lot of the work was "street" work and, according to Les, "That came easy to me. The street is where I grew up and I knew how to be in that environment." Later Les applied for a special unit in which he was doing undercover work for 14 months. "I bought drugs, guns, and other stuff on the street. We wanted to know not only who was involved, but how the various crime organizations were put together. I did a lot of coordination with the state police and the state's department of criminal investigation." After 14 months Les returned to the local police department and was back out on the "street." According to Les, "I now had a feel for what was going on. I was getting more comfortable in the role." He stayed there for the next four years.

About 1978, he became aware of a position opening for a crime scene technician with the state police. He applied, was accepted, and then attended various schools for training in areas such as firearms and latent prints. He then received an appointment to a 10 county region with the state police. According to Les, "I was extremely busy, and routinely did 40 hours or so of overtime a week. I felt I was getting better at this kind of work, but the pace was just too much." He eventually received some help and returned to school for more training. He learned how to "profile" a criminal, how to "read" a crime scene, and how to use photography. According to Les, "It became apparent that many law enforcement agencies really weren't prepared to do such investigation. And, different agencies had different agendas. What we needed was better coordination between city, county, and state agencies, along with courts, labs, and investigations." It also became apparent that investigators needed additional knowledge in areas like medicine. "The goal," according to Les, "was to be able to recreate the crime. But what was amazing, was how far off you could be if you weren't prepared to do the right kind of work. And this requires the right kind of training and experience."

How does a crime scene investigator do his/her job? According to Les, "It takes every skill you have to figure out how a crime occurred. The problem is, if you are not prepared to see something, then you will not likely see it. And, there isn't anything you can learn that won't someday prove valuable in some case. But it's much more than just observing. It's observing and thinking through what you are seeing. For example, when observing a person, what do you see? What you should be seeing are the culture, values, surroundings, and upbringing of people. They are all different, and on display, if you are ready to see them. When investigating a crime scene I try to put myself in the shoes of all involved. What did these people do? What was it that the killer, at a minimum, had to do?

As the investigation proceeds it is necessary to combine such thoughts with the appropriate tools. Sometimes you have to go out of your way to learn something. For example, Les has observed autopsies in order to learn more about how the body functions and reacts to certain circumstances and events. It is also important to pay attention to time. According to Les, "So many theories of what happened just don't hold any water because they fail the test of time. It's a simple idea, but a critical one. You must develop an ability to see the same scene from multiple perspectives. This isn't very easy for most because we are all a product of some perspective, which typically excludes other perspectives. This includes myself. That's one reason why I'm now taking an art class. What's interesting is that we all draw the same object or model. But because we see it from a different angle we see different things and our drawings differ." In this way Les has worked nearly 900 homicides in his career. This leads to one more critical ingredient, experience. In working on so many homicides over his career, Les has made it a point to learn from each one. For example, according to Les, "25% of the time in a homicide you'll talk to the killer in the initial investigation." Knowing this, and other lessons of experience, causes you to pay attention in a way not knowing leaves you ill prepared.

The kind of work Les does is not generally available within every law enforcement department. Therefore, according to Les, it is very important to carefully manage the interagency relationships. It is most often the case that some local police or sheriff's department officer is first on the scene, and they will tend to have a sense of ownership over the scene. Because of this, according to Les, "You have to be careful in how you approach them and your job. The secret to cooperation is to give everyone a role, or assignment. By doing so everyone has a responsibility and a particular involvement." Besides soothing emotions and smoothing relationships this plan, according to Les,". . . serves to protect the crime scene." While not in every case, it has happened that critical evidence has been inadvertently destroyed by officers unfamiliar with certain aspects of preserving the scene.

As can be seen, the needs and processes of investigation are diverse and potentially complicated. What then, should students now be doing to prepare? According to Les, students should by all means complete their education. Les did finish his AA degree, but has not gone on. He has however, continued to take many hours of training. "Everything in your education will be potentially valuable to you in this line of work. However, you need more than information. You should dig beneath the surface and learn the story underneath. You need to find out the hidden connections in any discipline. Dig! You also need to learn how to separate yourself from personal involvement in the crime; you need some emotional distance. Homicides are awful and if you let yourself get too involved you can't really do the job." For students in college this suggests developing a kind of detachment in research. Learn to argue a point without getting personally involved. Take a point of view which is opposite to yours and learn to argue it. You are not learning to be disingenuous, you are learning to protect yourself and your research. As for specific courses Les hesitates to be detailed. This is due to his position that all courses have potential value. But he does suggest the following. "Students should take a broad array of subjects, including courses in human behavior, law enforcement, computers, basic medicine or anatomy, and math--for the thought process."

In summary, Larry and Les demonstrate that solving crime requires a broad array of skills, perspectives and relationships. Crime scene investigation is both a science and an art. You are dealing with people often at their most emotional and irrational. And you are in settings of great tragedy and horror. Yet there is supreme satisfaction in solving a crime, a homicide, and bringing a murderer to justice. For this kind of work Larry and Les are well compensated, ranging from $65,000 - $70,000 annually, including overtime.

15

FEDERAL PROBATION

Glen Marley is the Chief U. S. Probation officer for a major metropolitan district in the Midwest. His responsibilities include both pre- and post-trial services. According to Glen, "You have to be able to, and want to, work with people. Obviously, many of those I work with are hard to like. However it is necessary to get to know each person individually so that the courts can make the right determination about their case and their lives. Ultimately you want the person in your care to become a contributor, rather than a detriment to society."

Glen's educational history presents a rather clear-cut model for students interested in a career in probation. In 1968 he completed a bachelor's degree with majors in sociology and psychology and a minor in geology. Of special significance during these undergraduate years, according to Glen, was the opportunity to intern. "As an intern I took positions at youth camps, city jails, and child and family services. These were important times in my development because it made the abstract real. The classroom concepts came alive and I could see the connections between the concepts and the realities of people's lives. It was also during these experiences that I became especially interested in corrections." The only problem was that the state in which Glen then lived had a hiring freeze in his field by the time he had graduated.

Consequently, after graduation Glen followed his wife's job prospects to the Midwest. While she worked in the business field Glen took a county job in welfare services. "During the next two years, I learned the in's and out's of the family welfare system. In particular, I became familiar with the problems of children, as that was the focus of my caseload. One prominent aspect of children on welfare is crime, and I became thoroughly familiar with the juvenile court system." After two years Glen took the civil services exam, scored well, and went to work for the county's adult probation program. At the same time Glen enrolled at a local university. After four years of work and school he had earned the Master's in Social Work (MSW) degree. There are two important themes emerging at this particular time in Glen's career. First, in the six years of Glen's employment he encountered nearly all there was in county corrections. "I got to see the systems inside and out. As much as anything I got to know the people involved and how they did their jobs. That kind of experience was invaluable. It was not something I could have acquired in the classroom." The second theme was the changing trends in corrections. According to Glen, "In the 1970's corrections was dominated by a medical model. Rehabilitation was the goal and this required certain kinds of concepts and skills. For this reason an advanced degree, like the MSW, was really appropriate. Not only did it teach me the model, but it also helped with the criteria for access to promotion within the federal system."

Ultimately, the system of corrections and its clients are comprised of people working together; that is, relationships. Though the relations may be hostile, they nonetheless are relations and must managed. For these reasons people skills are of the utmost importance. For example, a relationship between officer and client characterized by distrust will likely result in the most limiting of recommendations for the client. One such category of post-trial investigations is the measure of potential for rehabilitation of the person convicted of a crime. Low levels of trust may result in high expectations for client failure. This could, in turn, tend toward more restrictive sentencing (i.e., jail time verses probation). Likewise, the relationship between the probation officer and the court is critical. A good relationship is almost always necessary to produce an agreement on bail or sentencing. These are simply things that cannot be quantified, yet they have had a profound influence on the lives of countless individuals, and their families and friends. It is one of those "soft" skills that produces very concrete results.

After four years of experience and a graduate degree Glen moved from county probation to federal probation. In 1972 the federal justice system developed a new district in probation and Glen took a position as a caseworker. In 1985 he became Chief of the District. During the intervening time Glen redeveloped his justice system relationships, including judges, state's attorneys, and law enforcement officers, such as the local and state police, and the FBI. His personal network among such participants has been critical to his success. According to Glen, "I seldom have contested recommendations in court. There is an important level of trust between myself, the judge, prosecutors, and others involved. Without this you are left wondering just where you stand."

Just what kinds of work are involved? According to Glen, a great variety. Pre- and post-trial investigations provide different kinds of information. Pre-trial investigations check into the background of the person charged. Items evaluated include, but are not limited to, determination of indigent status, potential for flight (failure to show for trial), bail recommendation, and danger to society. According to Glen, "It is very important to treat everyone individually and fairly. This is sometimes difficult, but never less necessary to the integrity of the system." Post-trial investigations focus on appropriate levels of sentencing and the potential for rehabilitation. "You have to make 'judgment calls' because people's lives are just not black and white. And, there isn't a way to measure everything. On the other hand, individuals are not random in their behavior. They do have tendencies, and you learn to read these tendencies. It's obviously not an exact science, but you have to do what you can." In spite of the nature of this work (judgment calls and reading tendencies), Glen believes that, "We are moving away from a medical model of rehabilitation and towards a more mathematical model of punishment." Whether this is a sound model or effective way to go remains to be seen.

Aside from court cases Glen's staff also prepares plans for federal correctional institution releases. Given the nature of confinement, and the more recent trends towards punishment, prisoners released from correctional institutions are quite unprepared for civilian life. Caseworkers attempt to transition those paroled into independent living and work. However, according to veteran officers (who most likely came from the medical model), the emphasis today is too much on the protection of society and risk intervention. Control is the objective. The problem is that control does not easily translate to transition or change.

Today Glen oversees a staff of 30 with 15 officers. Each officer is responsible for all aspects of a particular case. In a recent year Glen's staff worked a total of approximately 230 cases. Of these, a little over 90% were sent to prison with just over 9% receiving probation. Typically about 14% of criminals convicted in federal court were sentenced to probation; 84% eventually plead guilty. Crack cocaine is involved in 61% of the cases. The high rate of imprisonment is indicative of the prevailing mathematical model.

In Glen's district there has generally been longevity in the job. As noted earlier, such longevity is ultimately important for the development of necessary experiences and networks within the criminal justice system. According to Glen, they have averaged 72 applicants for each opening. Of these 23 are tested and three are eventually interviewed. However, new trends may be altering this pattern.

So, what must one do to become one of the three? According to Glen, a variety of preparations are helpful. At the top of the list is the internship. As mentioned, the emphasis in federal law enforcement has moved to what Glen calls the mathematical model. The emotional emphasis of the politicians and the public is on law and order and punishment. One result is determinant sentencing. Another is harsher prison circumstances (i.e. removal of some education programs, or "luxuries" such as gyms and exercise equipment). Taken together, and along with shrinking fiscal resources, Glen feels that potential caseworkers possess shorter and shorter work histories. Because of this, according to Glen, "I have become more cautious in hiring. I look for those with internship experience. Over the last 10 years I've had 13 plus interns, and all but one have gone on to work for county, state or federal probation offices, or have otherwise stayed in criminal justice."

In terms of education Glen suggests the social and behavioral sciences. Bachelor's degrees are required, at a minimum, and master's degrees may be preferred for some positions. According to Glen half of the caseworkers in probation now have master's degrees. The one mitigating criterion is experience. According to Glen, "An MA with two years of experience is probably not as desirable as a BA with 10 years of experience." Such an emphasis provides some insight as to whether the potential caseworker can develop the necessary relationships to do the job and be effective. Other emerging qualities include computer literacy and skill in another language, particularly Spanish. Some districts will even pay a premium for bilingual officers.

Glen advises that a decent living can be made. Recently program budgeting has become decentralized with more local authority over expenditures. Experienced officers can expect pay in the neighborhood of $40,000 - $45,000, plus benefits. Entry level officers can expect pay in the neighborhood of $24,000, plus with benefits. And, according to Glen, men and women should apply. At present men comprise approximately 60% and women 40% of the workforce. Persons from minority populations are also encouraged to think about such careers. However, Glen is clear in stating that besides the details of degree and experience, the decision to hire comes down to an answer to the question. "How will they get along with staff and offenders? This is a people business."

16

VIOLENT CRIMES TASK FORCE

Dan Hunter is now 51 years old and a Master Sergeant in the state police. His primary focus has been a law enforcement entity called the Violent Crime Task Force. Originally federally funded and now regionally supported the task force focused on the kind of crimes most people fear, homicide. The task force worked both on investigation and prosecution of violent crime from organized gangs to random acts. According to Dan, "Working on the Violent Crimes Task Force has been a highlight of my career. Among other things I've had the opportunity to work with other agentcies on old unsolved homicides. It is really very satisfying to close a case that has been like an open wound to the family and friends of a victim." During the four years the task force was in effect as a federal entity, 115 arrests were made, 70 for first degree murder. The crimes solved had been on the books from two to twenty-four years. "We even solved a case which had been unsolved since 1961. Without this unit there would have been proven criminals walking the streets, many of them multiple killers." The federal grant ran out after four years and work now continues under the heading of the major case squad. Obviously Dan believes he has done important work, and the facts bear this out. So how does one come to do such service for the community?

Dan graduated from college in 1970 with a major in history. At that time the federal government had passed legislation generally referred to as the Safe Streets Act. Through this legislation the Law Enforcement Assistance Administration (LEAA) was established. This agency funded a wide array of law enforcement and crime fighting initiatives across the nation. In some instances new programs in criminal justice studies at universities were established, in other instances, states created mechanisms for the distribution of funds to local police departments for training, equipment, and personnel, as well as citizen groups for safe neighborhoods. In still other cases, states created new agencies. It was in this latter case that Dan began a career that has spanned nearly 30 years. The same year he graduated from college the state where he lived created a bureau of investigation. Dan had begun to develop an interest in criminal justice issues, as these were major national concerns at that time. So, he decided to pursue career options in that field. Through another federal program Dan was enrolled in a master's degree program in criminal justice, graduating in 1976. In the intervening time Dan completed the state police academy and had gone to work for the state's bureau of investigation.

For seven years, including the time he was in graduate school, Dan worked as an undercover agent in the southern half of the state. According to Dan, "I was young and motivated, and the job was both exciting and stressful. It was actually fascinating because you were learning how to fit in with all kinds of people. Knowing the law was one thing, but understanding people was really the most important skill. I had to dress the part and talk the part. In those days we were focusing on narcotics and other drug related crime, as well as organized crime in general. This meant that I typically had long hair and a beard, and I had to learn how to 'rap.' That's what we called it then, and while it would sound kind of silly today there is still a kind of 'rap,' it's just different. Basically you had to sell yourself to those involved in crime. You especially had to gain their confidence. This not only provided you with access to information which was ultimately necessary to your case, but it protected you. You had to be believable. If not, you, or your undercover colleagues, could be in jeopardy, let alone wasting your time. You see, in undercover work the final product is your testimony in court. This differs from the usual focus on evidence which you would have in investigating a homicide. You have to be, as nearly as possible, one of them, in order to know this culture and how they work. Finally, it was stressful. I was on the road a lot. Eventually you have to move on. It's not possible to be on undercover indefinitely. You run the risk of being discovered."

As was mentioned, Dan was in a graduate program at the same time as his undercover work. He felt that this was especially interesting in light of his classes. "I was able to see both the academic and applied sides of the issues we studied. In this way, I think I was really able to get the most out of the program."

After seven years Dan transferred to another part of the state where he worked on a different kinds of criminal activity for the bureau of investigation. Here he developed a wider array of investigating skills. In particular, he began to catch up on the latest investigatory technologies. For example, these now include DNA research and automated finger printing. Such technologies are important in several different ways. On the one hand it certainly helps in making specific cases against specific criminals. It also helps law enforcement in some ways stay ahead of the criminals. It is not possible to be everywhere and crime is likely to take place where law enforcement is absent. However, new developments in technology allow law enforcement to deter some crime. Of course, criminals learn and their tactics evolve, and technologies are generally known and available. It is just that crime fighting research has promoted our abilities in investigation, and technology is one important tool.

After a couple of years the state's bureau of investigation and the state police were merged. As much as anything this was a matter of finances. While Dan saw some positives, such as a larger force or manpower, the merger was full of challenges. His new role was that of crime scene analyst, and he had standing as an officer of the state police. The biggest challenge, according to Dan, ". . . was a new concept of organization. I had spent about 9 years learning law enforcement according to one kind of system. I knew what my objectives were, and I knew the people in the agency. You must understand that whether you are doing undercover, as I used to do, or you are working as an investigator, it is a matter of teamwork. You have to be able to coordinate well with others. Sometimes investigations proceed smoothly and at other times it is more halting, with information coming in all at one time or not at all. Because of this it is really very helpful to have others you can rely on whenever you need specialized input. So, it helps to know people well. In the old bureau

I knew others and others knew me. Now, merged with the state police, I had to learn not only new systems, but also new people." The fact is, crime is always inconvenient for investigation. And no matter how much the organization might try, it is impossible for everyone to know everything about crime scene analysis. It has even been known that law enforcement officers unfamiliar with certain investigatory needs, have inadvertently complicated the process, or even destroyed evidence. For example, timing can be all important, but a slow response could result in bad weather destroying a crime scene.

According to Dan, "This work involves a lot of agency overlap. People are territorial, and other law enforcement officers are people, so you must develop productive people skills. In some ways my years on undercover sharpened those skills. Just as I had to be able to 'rap,' I now have to be able to have rapport. Good relations are essential. Even if I believe, or in fact know for sure that I am right about a situation and others are wrong (or just uninformed), I cannot just take over an investigation. I must work with the others involved. The skills here are common sense and an ability and the insights necessary for communication. You have to ask, rather than tell, inform instead of conceal, and be part of the team instead of appearing to be an elite. In other words, just be careful."

Dan spent most of the next dozen years working specifically within the state police system, learning its ways and people. In 1992 the Violent Crime Task Force was created through another federal grant. For four years Dan was back in the kind of investigating environment in which he had begun. Dan's opinion on this time as a career "highlight" is already documented. The focus here is on the evolving nature of law enforcement. Recall the developments in law enforcement technology. But this is just one aspect. Dan's whole career has been significantly influenced by development, change, and opportunity. For example, Dan graduated just after the federal government began distributing major amounts of money into new law enforcement programs, which produced new agencies and resources. So, Dan went to work for a new state bureau of investigation and was put through school by means of a law enforcement education initiative. So it was in 1992 that Dan again rode the coattails of another new initiative-- the Violent Crime Task Force. Such is the nature of law enforcement. As Dan says, "There are all kinds of government grants, in particular federal grants, out there for the taking. What you need is an awareness of them, a recognition of their potential value, and a willingness to write for them. In my work, proposals are written nearly every month. This means that agencies and communities will vary in their ability to fight crime. It is not an even distribution of law enforcement resources across the board. But this is just the nature of the system. You need to know where the opportunities are and how to take advantage of them. If you don't, you will fall behind."

The grant for the Violent Crime Task Force soon ran its course, but Dan still works at the mission of the task force, only in new ways. "We still work as a unit, but more informally. There is no special name for our unit, but people know about us and we are called in when our expertise can be of help. We also work with the metropolitan area's major case squad. One change is fewer older cases and more immediate ones. Being more informal as a unit actually requires more comprehensive communication and organization skills. You have to have a lot of personal contacts. You must be cooperative and flexible."

So, what should students be thinking of doing now, if Dan's career holds interest for them. "The first thing is to follow your interests." Dan wants it known that, "There is great diversity within law enforcement. There are all kinds of special units. So it is possible to access law enforcement by a wide variety of means. Pursue whatever interests you have. However, be sure to gain experience." As with his advanced studies, Dan felt he learned so much more in class when he had relevant experiences as a point of departure and comparison.

While the state police academy generally requires only two years of college, the four-year degree is becoming a much more common expectation. Competition will make it nearly required. Related to this is the need for more wide-ranging means of communication. For example, foreign languages are necessary in all metropolitan areas. Some departments may even require it of new hires. Dan has seen real growth in needs for Spanish and Asian language skills. In another vein, Dan recommends strong writing skills. This is especially necessary if grant writing is to be a tool by which resources are accessed. This in turn presumes a basic knowledge of computers. And, an extension of this is data management. You must know how to access and manipulate data. Finally, "You must, above all else, know how to get along with and understand people. To fail in this regard is to fail to get the job done." Think of those 115 arrests, with 70 for first degree murder, without such skills.

17

CITY POLICE OFFICER

Alex Mosly is now a police department lieutenant in a major west coast metropolitan area. The challenges are as diverse as over 150 language groups represented in the population, intense crowding of people in living quarters and traffic, and great disparities in socio-economic class. As an officer, Alex must be oriented both to service to the community and administration of the department. To this end, Alex says that ". . . the number one skill is communication! Ninety percent of what I do, and what any police officer does, is communication, orally or in writing. You write reports, interview suspects and victims, intervene in hostile situations, testify in court, and even give speeches." If you cannot communicate you cannot possibly do the job of a police officer.

Alex began his journey to a career in law enforcement in the early 1970's. After high school he attended college and majored in criminal justice. Such majors were relatively new on the scene, due significantly to the influx of federal grant dollars. However, Alex, ". . . can't really explain my interest in criminal justice. I knew that I wanted to get a job where I could help people. Actually, my focus on criminal justice was developed probably as much through the form of education I was receiving as anything else. The college I attended employed a co-op based program. What you did was take classes for six months of the year and then worked in a course-related co-op assignment for the next six months." One such related assignment was in the field of industrial security. Alex served in a supervisory capacity. While not law enforcement per se, it nonetheless is a related field, one in which a number of law enforcement personnel from across the country regularly serve.

Alex's junior year was a turning point in terms of focus. As mentioned, Alex's choice of criminal justice, while a point of interest, was not yet a commitment. In fact, he had begun thinking about pursuing a law degree. However, according to Alex, "I really didn't score well enough on the LSAT." While this certainly could have been seen as a setback, Alex responded by refocusing on law enforcement and began taking more police oriented courses. "I had already taken criminal justice theory courses, but I lacked the practical and detailed knowledge of police work."

At the same time, Alex began exploring the employment opportunities in his native east coast urban home. "What I found was that, at least in that area, the route to a law enforcement job traveled through a series of political connections. You had to have a connection in order to get the job." On the other hand, according to Alex, "I saw the west coast as much more politically free. Hiring and appointments were based on testing and merit. In addition, states such as California required a two-year degree." This suggested that the job could be earned, rather than distributed as political patronage.

By 1977, Alex was completing his BS in criminal justice and at the same time actively looking for a job. "Altogether this was about a six month process. I determined that I should look for work at home and on the west coast. I was eventually offered a position as a part-time reserve officer in a west coast metropolitan area community. I also attended the police academy 20 hours a week." For about year Alex worked and learned west coast law enforcement via both the academy and employment. In 1979, he made application to the nearby community where he now serves as a lieutenant in the police department.

Alex has an interesting perspective on the relationship of his education to his job search and the first stages of employment. "My degree in criminal justice certainly did open some doors for me. It gave me access where access was based on education and merit. If the department where I now work had been more politically driven, then the degree would have been of less value in this respect. I should say, however, that in a technical sense my degree did not really make me a better officer. Experience is what makes you a better officer. But there were valuable contributions which must not be overlooked. My education taught me something about people and their relationships, particularly how to work with others. This is a key point, in that law enforcement is not the work of an individual. It is the work of many in cooperation. My degree made me a more well-rounded person. I learned that there were a variety of perspectives held by people around the world, and I learned how to entertain them. It is very easy to dismiss points of view with which you are unfamiliar. This is dangerous to police work, but also dangerous to any kind of cooperative tasks. I would even say that without an education a person will tend to see the world myopically. Finally, there are the skills rather than the perspectives. An education prepares you to test better, speak better, and interview better. Many times a person who otherwise would be an excellent officer, nonetheless tests poorly, speaks poorly, and interviews poorly. They can't get through the door to the opportunity beyond. Education, in this respect, is invaluable."

After taking a full time position as a police officer in 1979, Alex embarked on still a new learning experience. According to Alex, "As a first line officer I worked the streets and learned. I also attended two academies, one for 500 hours (three days a week for six months) and one for 1,000 hours (five to six days a week for six months). I learned more specific laws, such as criminal, vehicular, and narcotics. I learned the specific day-to-day operations of a field officer. And I was constantly challenged, academically, mentally, and physically." From 1979 until 1984, Alex was a first line officer, and developed his skills and perspectives.

By 1984 Alex was ready to move on with his career, as he took and passed the Sergeant's exam. Alex believes that his ". . . BS degree was really helpful. I had learned good study skills and tested well. I had learned how to speak and present myself and I therefore interviewed well. I was prepared practically and academically. And, I had to be prepared to see law enforcement, and the police department in different ways. I had to have a bigger picture of the department, I had to

71

exercise communication skills and an administrative perspective, and I had to deal with new issues."

One particular new issue was the fact that Alex ". . . broke through the ceiling of traditional police organizations. I was the first officer to make Sergeant based on merit, not time and experience. I was faced with the fact that I was a five year officer, and now a Sergeant, with authority over first line officers with 20 years of experience. I addressed this by making sure that in whatever I was doing, especially if it involved change or specific use of authority, I consulted with senior officers. By asking their opinions, I demonstrated that I valued their ideas, experience, and input. Exercising authority alone would simply not work. This is, again, an area where I believe my education with its emphasis on communication and people skills, has really paid off."

Alex's value for education was energized in his new position and he subsequently enrolled in an MA program in Public Administration and Policy. While nonetheless working full-time, Alex completed the degree by 1987. Such a focus is understandable in light of the size and scope of the department which has 152 sworn officers and 216 employees in total. With any organization this size, change is inevitable. This fact demanded Alex's attention, it is also very instructive to students considering a career in police work. In his approximately 20 years in police departments, Alex says, "The most significant change is the evolution of the 'me' generation. This has really been apparent in the last 10 years. The evidence of it is a sense of entitlement. The idea that we are somehow owed our position and benefits. Merit begins to take a back seat. New officers especially have this sense of 'me.' As a result, many of these officers are unable to see the larger picture. They have difficulty seeing the interconnections of the department as a whole, and how that department fits into the still larger community. Further evidence of this can be seen in the living patterns of officers. Many now live 20-40 miles away. This breaks down essential relationships and helps produce a sense of being disconnected. Ultimately, it can and does lead to a loss of *esprit de corps*." Alex suggests that those considering careers in police work need to understand that their work is absolutely dependent upon the work of fellow officers. And, they should work towards developing these relationships. Failure to do so results in failure of the departmental mission.

After completing the MA in 1987, Alex was on the move within the department, both figuratively and actually. In 1987, he transferred to the traffic division where he became a motorcycle Sergeant and supervised motorcycle officers for two years. In 1988, he tested for lieutenant but was not promoted. He tested again in 1989, and was promoted. His salary went from about $55,000 per year to $75,000 per year, plus benefits. This was certainly a positive aspect of Alex's rise in the department. But, Alex is also motivated by other values, including education and a commitment to the community at large.

According to Alex, "The master's degree definitely, without a doubt, helped in my understanding of the difference between supervision and management. I believe I have better organizational relationships and I have better insights into what makes people behave the way they do. The graduate degree has also impacted my standing and credibility within the community. At the very least it has opened doors that might otherwise have remained closed, or been more difficult to open. I am able to have more of a peer or colleague relationship with other personnel in the city who also have advanced degrees. Many such people don't think of a police officer as having advanced degrees, and when they find that out about me I get an immediate boost in credibility. This is

important as my work now takes me into matters throughout the community, matters not typically thought of as police business. These would include finance, recruitment, strategic planning, and design related to roads and infrastructure. For example, we are now designing traffic flow patterns which could result in a person being able to drive at 35 m.p.h. across the entire city without having to stop for a light. With traffic being such a high priority, and a source of frustration for so many, it is important to be able to better manage it. We call it 'traffic calming.' But the point is, such an effort intersects with so many other departments and personnel of the city, as well as contact with civilians of the city. Knowing how to negotiate all these relationships is important to success."

So, how should students in college now be preparing for a future career in law enforcement? According to Alex, there are many meaningful steps. "First, you need to understand that law enforcement is a continuing education process. Each job you might do has a specific area of knowledge with which you must be familiar. But in addition, as with the idea of traffic calming, those same specific areas continue to evolve and change. Knowing something now is no guarantee of knowing enough in the future. So, you must be receptive to on-going training." Regarding degrees Alex says, "It really doesn't matter what degree you earn. It matters that you earn a degree. The degree says something about your discipline, commitment, and values." But there are areas which you should explore or at least experience. According to Alex, these include, ". . . developing excellent writing skills, particularly your ability to write clear and accurate reports. Work on your ability to make presentations. Learn to give speeches. You must be able to carry yourself orally. Second languages really open doors. In some cases hiring will specifically require proficiency in a language like Spanish or Vietnamese. Related to this is cultural awareness. You must be generally aware of the fact that there are many different cultures represented in the community. And, it helps to know specific details of at least some. Become observant of people. Learn how they behave. Become an active listener. There is more at issue than just what is being said. Learn to become a professional, and conduct yourself as one."

This certainly seems like a long list, and in some ways it is. But the career you are considering is one full of responsibility. As civilians we have high expectations of law enforcement personnel. According to Alex, these high expectations are evident in the community's investment in them as officers. Including wages and benefits, Alex's department invests about $100,000 to produce a first line officer. However, the investment does not begin paying dividends at the time of appointment. According to Alex, "In the first year the new officer is primarily going through intensive training. In the second year the officer is learning how the classroom and the field come together in experience. In years three through five the officer develops both organizational and independent abilities. He/she learns to make decisions. At this point the department begins to realize the first value for its investment." As you can now see, this is serious business, and it requires equally serious commitment.

18

COUNTY SHERIFF

Jason Green was elected county sheriff four years ago at the age of 29. He was then and continues to be the youngest county sheriff in his Midwestern state. While this may be somewhat unusual, it was not unexpected in the case of Jason. You see, Jason was the fourth county sheriff in his family. According to Jason, "I was surrounded by role models but not just within my family. For me there were a number of local law enforcement people who were role models for me. I looked up to them." One result was that by the eighth grade Jason had decided that he would somehow pursue a career in law enforcement. " I have always liked working with people and I also had a desire for public service. Law enforcement was a natural for me."

After high school Jason attended a local junior college for one and one-half years. While there he took both general education and law enforcement related courses. Before graduating, however, Jason took a local police department development test and was hired on his 21st birthday, at $5.35 per hour to start. He stayed with the department for just nine months when he transferred to the local sheriff's department. He earned $4,000 more per year there and stayed with the force for two years. However, work in a rural area, and on a small force was financially difficult, and after two years he quit and sold cars for a year.

For someone with as much law enforcement "in his blood" as Jason, he could not long stay in the civilian work force. After a year dealing cars Jason was recruited to deal drugs! This requires a little explanation. Jason was recruited and hired by a former law enforcement contact to do undercover work. This he did for a multi-jurisdictional drug task force. To prepare for this Jason was enrolled in a two week Drug Enforcement Administration undercover school. The emphasis was almost purely sociological. According to Jason, "You need to be able to observe and study people, and you have to be able to adopt a different mind set. You have to learn to think and be like a drug dealer. You need to become a part of that setting." Simply put, if you cannot accurately assess, and then effectively adopt a new role, you cannot be undercover. But Jason was able to do just that. He even pierced his own ear. The work was both stressful and exciting. One of the stresses was that he was leading a double life. According to Jason, ". . . this just wasn't normal. There were times when I felt somewhat confused about my identity." But Jason was able to figure it out. He managed this double life for two years. "It was satisfying," according to Jason. "You could see immediate results from your work." But two years was enough for Jason and his family.

Eventually Jason returned to the police department for which he had originally worked. For a little over three years, Jason readjusted to a more normal identity while still pursuing his passion. Based on his work in drug enforcement Jason assumed responsibility for the local DARE program. Other than that Jason worked as a patrol officer until 1994. During this time Jason was reconsidering his future in law enforcement. He was coming to the conclusion that he would make a run for sheriff. "I knew that I was young, but I also had experience. I had not only been working in the field for most of the last eight years, but I had basically grown up in law enforcement, particularly the sheriff's role. But I also thought I had some ideas to offer the community." In 1994 Jason was elected sheriff, the fourth member of his extended family to hold that office. According the Jason, "I had just entered a whole new world; that of politics." For Jason the first realization was the amount of time the political side of the job would take. "Election years are especially time consuming. You are doing all kinds of things which you don't typically associate with law enforcement. This includes knocking on doors, putting up signs, campaigning at dinners, service clubs, fairs, etc." Another characteristic of campaigning is that in a small town or rural area, the politics seem less partisan. That is, people are more interested in who you are, not your political party. "What people want is to be able to talk to their elected officials."

After the election Jason found that the intense interpersonal nature of campaigning did not necessarily let up once he was on the job. It still mattered to people that they have a sense of contact with those they have elected. According to Jason, "The work is never just what I do at the office. In fact it is much more continuous than my days in undercover. Now the work actually follows me home. People frequently call me at home, at all hours. While I accept this as part of the job, I must learn to manage this if I am to have any kind of family life."

Aside from constituent relations the sheriff's position is required to engage in a number of collateral relations. The sheriff is asked to show up at any number of local events. He is also responsible to local government and regional entities, as well as other law enforcement and correctional agencies. He must also serve the force's administrative function. Included is local jail management, courthouse security, and labor negotiations with the Fraternal Order of Police. This is in addition to the normal job of community law enforcement. According to Jason, "Each and every day brings something new and different to do. But the one thing in common is that nearly all these responsibilities are built around interpersonal relationships. The job works only if the relationships work. This makes your network of law enforcement and social contacts all the more important."

Now Jason is again in campaign season. Actually, according to Jason, "I tend to run a bit scared. You just never know what the next day will bring. In fact I began preparing for this year's election nearly two years ago." One thing which Jason knows all too well is that what worked when he was a minimum wage police officer twelve years ago likely does not work, at least in the same way, now. "Things change," according to Jason, "even in a small community. If you stand still then things will pass you by. For example we think of drugs as an urban problem, and it is a problem in the cities. But that doesn't mean it hasn't become a problem in rural areas. It has, but in different ways. We are located on a major interstate which is, among other things, a conduit for drug traffickers. And we find drugs being produced in the countryside, such as meth labs and cultivation of marijuana."

So, where do we go from here? According to Jason, where we go has as much to do with your perspective as your actions. "We must develop a proactive rather than a reactive stance to our issues. As an example, while the DARE program has generally been a positive program it is necessary to review it. Doing no harm is not the same as doing good. We have to consider, how contemporary is it? What may have worked for an elementary age student at eight may no longer work for that same student as an eighteen year old high school senior. We also need to continuously upgrade our skills, tools, and information. We must always be in training, for the present and the future."

The proactive perspective is critical for students considering working as a sheriff. Among other things Jason has decided to keep working at his associate's degree. But the days are numbered for those without a four-year degree. In part this is due to the knowledge and array of skills which are now becoming a must. According the Jason, law enforcement agencies are now looking for students with a background, if not a degree, in the social sciences. Whatever else the sheriff's job is, it requires an ability to read and relate to a widening array of persons and situations. But do not overlook the value of a good general education. The variety of courses across disciplines develops the perspectives necessary to see issues from different points of view. Specific skills now include writing for reports of all kinds, computer skills, and in a growing number of areas, bilingual capabilities. There are also powerful initiatives for the development of women and minorities. You must be able to speak, not only to an emotional citizen, but children and the media. You are often called upon to give speeches or other public talks.

For all of this, including running a department with sixteen full-time and five part-time officers, Jason receives a state-scheduled minimum annual salary of $38,000-plus. While this obviously is not equal to the amounts of money of his peers across the state, Jason does not complain. "The benefits are good and it does fit, somewhat, the cost of living in a small town. In conclusion, Jason offers the following point of view. "Law enforcement officers today should be thinking about the future and using their position to better society for our kids. Law enforcement must adopt a positive outlook on society and see its primary responsibility as helping people."

19

COUNTY AND REGIONAL
COMMISSIONER

Tom Francis has and continues to perform in a number of different positions. He has held a diverse array of roles in his almost 70 years. Most prominently he has been an ordained pastor, a college professor, and politician and county board member. According to Tom, "I have always been interested in the Republican Party, and I am an activist." While he approached his interests in different ways in his early life, it was in 1974 when Tom became a Republican Party precinct committeeman. In 1976 a local county board member resigned. Since his term was unexpired, the law required a same-party candidate be nominated to fill the vacancy. Tom was nominated by his precinct and ultimately approved to serve the remainder of the term. Later that year he was elected for a new four-year term, and he has served continuously in that capacity to the present.

According to Tom, "Serving on the county board takes you into all aspects of community life. You serve on board committees, you are asked to be a part of other committees and planning groups, and people simply seek you out to talk about what's on their minds." One example of this was Tom's appointment by the board chairman to a regional law enforcement commission encompassing seven counties. The commission was organized essentially as an administrative vehicle to apply for and distribute federal grant funds to sheriff's and police departments. The commission was comprised of elected officials from sponsoring county boards, elected sheriffs, police chiefs, and some other members of the public. Within the commission Tom has served as vice president, president, treasurer and acting executive director.

Through the commission regional law enforcement agencies were provided funded opportunities to develop their skills and capacities. By pooling resources agencies have had access to expertise which they could never have produced on their own. For example, the commission and the state's southern police chiefs' association combined forces to establish a training region. According to Tom, who was the first chairman of the training region, "The purpose of the training region was to provide short courses for police, sheriff's deputies, correctional officers, state police, dispatchers, executives in law enforcement and criminal justice generally, and others. Whatever else may be true about law enforcement one thing is certainly true, and that is the landscape of crime and how we deal with it continues to shift. Change is a fact. In some cases we have law enforcement officers with 10-20 year old equipment, and even older training, trying to keep up with crime as fast paced as the computer. They just didn't have a chance. The courses that we (the commission) offered brought state of the art knowledge to the officers."

Some of the specific areas the commission headed by Tom taught included the following. Officers were trained in the unique details of finding missing children. Related to this was training in the detection and prevention of child molestation. Another course prepared criminal justice personnel in the special problems of the aged, including protection from scams, promoting a clear understanding on the part of the elderly of their criminal justice rights, and more public awareness of elder abuse. The commission was assigned by the state to train sheriff's deputies in firearms. Courses were offered for defensive driving for police and ambulance drivers. 911 dispatchers were trained as well as DARE officers. Agencies were taught disaster management and communication. And agencies were instructed in the importance and value of good public relations, including the concept of being a public official. According to Tom, "The point is, that it is impossible for each and every agency of law enforcement to keep up with all the changes in the field of criminal justice. Our training region not only addresses the needs various departments say they have, but often some they don't know they have." An example of the latter is victim rights. While we know that victims have rights, we often do not seem to be aware of it at the moment of a crime. The result is victims too often get pushed aside as focus is brought to bear on the crime and criminal.

In fact, the list of needs for training is endless. As officers age and retire new officers must be trained to take their place. As criminals and crime take on new forms agencies must adapt. Two simple cases are the need for computer literacy for criminal justice personnel and, bilingual capabilities and cross cultural understanding. Among all the things criminal justice agencies do, they keep records. A real problem is accessing them when you need them. Computer technology is one answer, but without computer literate personnel records might as well be lost. New technologies also have the potential to enhance communication, or simply find persons and things through global satellite positioning.

On the culture front it is becoming obvious that criminal justice personnel must have some understanding or sensitivity to sub cultural structures and language if they are to be in a position to serve increasingly diverse populations. It is generally understood, for example, that by or before the middle of the next century (2050) over half the population of the United States will be people of color. This means that less than half the population will be Caucasian/white. This speaks to the potential for tremendous changes in how we construct and conduct community. For example, a major metropolitan area has, over the years, completed a major demographic shift from predominately white to predominately black. Those who have migrated out, however, have tended to settle in a collar of communities surrounding the city proper. These changes have caused obvious tensions in the enforcement of laws. Recently a kind of reverse "hate crime" has grabbed the headlines as a white youth was attacked by a group of black youths. In the midst of this major demographic change the metropolitan area has been further changed by the steady immigration of southeast Asian refugees. One response has been the hiring of the first Vietnamese speaking officer on the force. Such changes are inevitable and powerful.

Tom was, and continues to be at the heart of demographic/institutional change in his community. From 1986-1988, as county board chairman, he led the county's effort in convincing the Federal Bureau of Prisons to locate a new facility there. This was a tremendous, and occasionally controversial undertaking. On the one hand, it meant jobs and a significant economic boost to the surrounding economy. Not only would money flow in for construction and maintenance of such a facility, but people would move into the community thereby increasing the demand for housing, raising the tax base, etc. On the other hand, people were concerned about the social and perceptual impact of such a facility. Citizens worried that "the wrong kinds of people" (a subtle racial worry) could move into the area as they followed prisoners around the country. Others worried that they city would come to be overwhelmingly identified as a prison town, and that identity would make it somehow less appealing. To this end Tom was at the center of community education efforts to calm fears and bring reasoned thinking to the fore. Eventually the prison was built and is now simply a part, though not an overwhelming part, of the local community structure.

For his part Tom's work with the prison did not end with construction and startup. In 1995, he entered the Federal Correctional Institution Volunteer program. According to Tom, "What we have done is to create a program unique within the entire Federal Bureau of Prisons. It is a 'values' program, which is actually an outgrowth of the prison drug program. Our goal is to work towards a better understanding of values and ethics. Inmates in this program are screened for selection and are held to a particularly high standard for conduct. All men participating are housed together. However, failure to maintain the expectation of the program results in dismissal and a return to general prison population housing. Once a week for two hours I teach a course to 13-21 men on some aspect of values. We want them to learn to make good choices; to even recognize that they have choices." The course is wide-ranging with inmates studying classic writings and literature, which illustrate value issues in subjects such as philosophy and comparative religion. Interestingly, some time after Tom began this program a riot occurred at that prison. Damage was done and some people were injured (again, race discrimination was involved). In the aftermath the prison facility was "hardened," certain inmates were prosecuted, and many others were transferred to prisons of higher security. However, Tom's group of students did not participate. They stayed in their housing unit, avoiding all participation in the riot. And, they were the only housing unit to do so. Three years into the "Values" program, Tom was recently honored by the F.C.I. as "Volunteer of the Year."

Tom has brought a unique perspective and contribution to his sphere of criminal justice. He is not a professional in the field, in fact, he received no pay for his work in law enforcement other than a stipend for his work on the county board. Yet Tom says, "I have found my work on behalf of law enforcement incredibly satisfying." He is still an ordained minister and now a retired professor of religion and philosophy. And, this experience is what he brings to the tables of law enforcement. He is not a specialist, but in nearly 25 years of service, "I have come to learn a few things." Among these is the realization that, ". . . I do have something to contribute in a meeting of hard-nosed law enforcement officers. I bring a dimension of religious and philosophical thought to the issues at hand. There is never enough resource to go around and tensions can easily boil over. Sometimes just having me present keeps this from happening. And, by perhaps not being the expert, or the one with a specific vested interest, I can turn the problem in such a way as to see solutions not before noticed."

The point in this profile is that criminal justice is addressed in so many different ways. While Tom has not been trained himself in firing a weapon, he has seen to it that those who might, or must, have had the best training available. And then, Tom goes a step further. He is an advocate for the officer who has had to use his weapon. It can be traumatic, shooting and possibly killing another person. The officer needs tending. Tom believes in the chaplains programs. Further, it is often the officer who must break the news to families of a death. Not only is this hard for families to hear, but it is hard for officers to do.

Some would not call Tom's work exactly a career. Others would. In any case, how do you prepare to be as impactful as Tom? Tom offers a list of things to be considering while still in school. "First, become thoughtful people and learn about people. Get a four year liberal arts degree. Take courses especially in fields like, history, philosophy, ethics, sociology, anthropology, and psychology. These fields will help you not only understand human behavior, which is critical to the work of criminal justice, but will help you understand yourself. You need to develop patience and wisdom. You need to do internships, because this is the area where your ideas and you yourself are tested. Ultimately, it is the development of a sound moral underpinning that will make the most difference. You must remember that you will be forced to make decisions in life, often quickly and sometimes in crisis. Such decisions will sometimes have life-long implications. So, be prepared, but broadly, not narrowly."

20

ALCOHOL, TOBACCO, AND FIREARMS

Austin Edward's father was an ATF (Alcohol, Tobacco, and Firearms) special agent, though he advised against Austin majoring in criminal justice while in college. While Austin was interested in criminal justice, his father was concerned with the potential narrowness of the degree. "What if you don't pursue a career in criminal justice, or don't like the work? What will you do then?" These were the cautionary questions Austin's father posed. But, according to Austin, "While growing up in a *Leave It To Beaver* family, I had the opportunity to see my father come home, day after day, from a job he loved." At that time he was a city police officer in a major metropolitan area. "I say my father as a role model, and I saw that he enjoyed his job. The pay always seemed enough to provide for the family. And, I recall thinking that this was the kind of work that I would probably want to do."

That role modeling extended to Austin's pursuit of a degree. When Austin was eleven his father began a night school program for a college degree. His degree earned was in the area of community and social services, not criminal justice. The decision to do this was for the express purpose of "bettering" opportunities for the family. It was in the process of attending two different community colleges and completing his degree at a four year institution, that Austin's father met an ATF special agent who was working on his masters degree. That agent advised him that the ATF would be hiring soon, and that with his degree and experience he should consider applying. Upon graduation Austin's father did apply and took a position in another city with the ATF. According to Austin, "This move was in the best interests of the family. It provided more money, and required fewer nights and weekends. It gave us more family time." It was also the case that Austin saw his father in a new light. Instead of wearing a uniform, he now wore a suit and tie. Instead of patrolling, his work tended towards investigation and occasional undercover work. But is was the family time that was most important. "I began to see that this kind of work gave us a chance at a normal family life, in addition to an interesting, even exciting kind of work." In retrospect, now with a family and career of his own, Austin sees what his father did with a new kind of respect. "His decisions, and the choices he made in the 70's made me who I am today. Had we stayed put, with my Dad staying in the local police force, we would have not made the moves we did, and consequently, my horizons would have been limited. Obviously, his choices have led to my opportunities now."

"While my father was the first in his family to go to college, it was different for me. There was never any doubt that I would go to college; only where and what I would study." But Austin was already making up his mind about criminal justice. "I knew that I was most likely going into this field. It was always in the back of my mind. And, it impacted my behavior. I'm not saying that I was perfect. I had my times. But I didn't want to mess up my future by doing anything too crazy. Kids need to know that what they do now can and will follow them later in life."

Actually, at the point of high school graduation Austin had developed a new interest in architecture, and for the first time began to waver in his commitment to criminal justice. In fact, Austin's father was very supportive of this new direction. So, Austin went off to college, on a baseball scholarship, with the intention of at least exploring architecture. According to Austin, "When I was enrolling for my first classes I was in introductory courses for both criminal justice and architecture. However, there was an extra cost for supplies for the architecture course and I couldn't afford it at that time. So, I substituted an additional criminal justice course in juvenile behavior." At the end of that first semester Austin's grades in the criminal justice courses were all very strong, while other courses were more average. According to Austin, "With those grades it was easy to see where my interests were. So, I followed that semester up with more criminal justice and sociology related courses. I knew then that this was what I wanted to pursue. It was a matter of studying what I found interesting and challenging. Something that made me want to learn. Further, I wanted to excel, not just get by. I felt that in criminal justice I could get the kind of GPA that would say to some agency that I was well prepared and ready for the job."

By the summer before his senior year Austin's father was accepting of the fact that Austin would be following in his footsteps. At the same time, it must be understood that Austin's relationship to the criminal justice profession generally, by way of his father, meant that he was well situated for connections. So, according to Austin, "My Dad said that if this was the direction I was going to go, then I needed to get on with some of the necessary steps. This included beginning to take the various exams which all law enforcement agencies require. For the ATF this meant taking the Treasury Enforcement Agent exam (TEA)." The same would have been required of the FBI, U.S. Marshals, and local police departments as well. The advice was that given the challenging nature of these exams, it would be to Austin's advantage to take them during his senior year. That way, if necessary, he could retake them at graduation. In Austin's case this meant taking the U.S. Marshal's exam and the TEA, which was the exam employed by ATF, Customs, Secret Service, and the Internal Revenue Service's Criminal Investigator's Division. He had also enrolled to test for a major metropolitan area police department. This was the fall of 1986, and on the heels of recent passage of major legislation regarding crimes with guns, drugs, etc. According to Austin, "Here I am, taking these exams for Federal law enforcement and these agencies are getting ready to hire. I couldn't have been more fortunate." Austin passed both the U.S. Marshal's test and the TEA that fall. The result is interviews with both Customs and ATF, the latter in his former home town.

In his interview with the ATF Austin was at least partially within the scope of his father's professional network. During the interview, however, Austin was told not to have his hopes up too high, given that the ATF preferred not to hire directly out of college. Instead, they would rather hire new agents who had some previous law enforcement experience. There were, however, other offices which were going to be hiring more agents due to the new fire arms related legislation recently enacted. The interview itself was a very structured affair, lasting three hours. According to Austin, "The first hour was basically an introduction to the ATF. Emphases were the responsibilities of an ATF agent, especially the legal and ethical expectations." The second hour focussed on Austin. Included were not only questions about his preparations, educationally and otherwise, but also rather simple questions about him as a person. According to Austin, "Some of the questions were of a general nature, such as why was I interested in the ATF. But others were very much to the point. These included scenarios which were designed to test my willingness to pursue the truth, even with my colleagues. They were not only looking for ethical responses to potentially difficult situations, but they were looking for qualities of character. Students should know that qualities like these speak to your ability to relate well, and work well with others. Questions were also asked about my own history related to drugs. The point is, if you are to be a federal agent you simply cannot break the law, even if you are undercover. Once you lose the quality of a clean reputation, you may never recover it. If this happens, then you simply cannot do your job. Actually, they are looking for a thoughtful response."

In the third hour Austin had to demonstrate another quality. In his case, he was asked to listen to an audio tape of a person reporting on a fire scene. Austin's job was to summarize the audio tape, in writing. According to Austin, "The summary had to be no more than two pages. They were essentially wanting to see if I had all the basics--who, what, when, where, why--in the report. It's kind of a paradox in this job. We need to have all relevant information in the report, but it can't be long and drawn out. You have to be able to keep it short, but still have everything included."

The interview process took place in December of 1986, and it is now January of 1987. Austin is not expecting an offer in his home town. Further, he had decided that if an offer did come, from the east or west coasts, he would probably not accept it. Rather, he had continued to pursue testing for the local police department, and had an offer to advance to the academy for training. At the same time, the ATF office at which he had interviewed had initially decided to recommend Austin to the Los Angeles office. However, the interview with ATF went extremely well, and Austin proved himself worthy. Austin graduated on May 15, 1987 and his job with ATF began May 24, 1987. "While I believe I was as prepared as I could have been, I also know that I was a fortunate individual." Austin is now a Special Agent for the ATF.

According to Austin, while he was grateful for the offer, and being an ATF agent was exactly what he wanted to be, he was nonetheless nervous as he approached his first day of work. According to Austin, "The day before my first day of work was a holiday, and I think I drove the route to work at least three times, just to make sure I knew how to get to the office, find parking, everything. I was a nervous wreck! But once that first day began I realized that I would be working with good people, and they wanted me to succeed." By 9:00 AM of the first day Austin had been taken before a judge and was sworn in as a special agent. He was then given a badge and credentials, though not a firearm. This reason for this was that it was required that he train and qualify first. Within a couple of days Austin had qualified. Austin was also assigned to a local supervisor known as an On the Job Trainer (OJT). For the next four weeks Austin worked with his OJT, learning the work, formal and informal, of a special agent. According to Austin, "We would go out three or four nights a week, to the local police and sheriff's departments. My OJT would introduce me around. He also introduced me to other federal agents in customs, the U.S. Marshals, etc. At that time the *hot* law enforcement trend was task forces. This meant that we had to be able to cooperate, to integrate our efforts. Without good working relationships with other departments and agencies, there would be no way to get the job done." Such relationships are absolutely critical when understood in context. According to Austin, in the past ten years he has served as the Case Agent on 18 arson and explosive investigations, responded to over forty arson and explosive scenes, and testified over 100 times in trials or other court proceedings. Without an ability to coordinate with other agencies and departments, there is simply no way to adequately pursue such a number of cases. It was then off to the Federal Law Enforcement Training Center (i.e., the academy).

The academy was eighteen weeks long, and was comprised of two separate parts. The basic academy was designed for the criminal investigators, and included everyone assigned to Treasury (the federal department to which ATF is assigned), including customs, IRS, secret service, ATF, Treasury Office of Internal Investigations, Labor Department Investigators, and Department of Transportation Investigators, among others. His class was comprised of approximately 48 students. The first nine weeks covered basic laws, such as search and seizure, handcuffing techniques, physical fitness, and how to safely proceed on felony car stops. "The point," according to Austin, "was to expose you to a little bit of everything."

After the first part of the academy was completed Austin then went to "new agent training." This was specific to ATF, with 24 new ATF agents in the class. The first two weeks was "all guns." New agents must learn all related gun laws, all firearm laws, all licensing laws. Then two weeks of arson laws, including everything related to fires, investigations, working with insurance agencies, record-keeping, etc. Next was explosives for two weeks, and finally undercover training. This was followed by about four days of practical exercises. "We were just trying to figure out how to put this all together. And of course, we were all ready to just hit the street and save the world!!" Of course, the senior agents, according to Austin, "...have to tone down our enthusiasm a bit."

In 1987 Austin's government salary rating was a GS-7, and he started at about $28,000 plus benefits. Today that translates to about $38,000. According to Austin, the comparison of ATF pay scales to local police or sheriff's deputies must take into consideration the opportunities for other sources of income. Many local law enforcement agents also have the opportunity for overtime, or even working security, or other special events. For ATF agents, this is not the case. Besides the different nature of the work and time demands, it is likely, according to Austin, that "you will have to move." This can put the family at risk. Austin feels that the long-term benefits are great, but the pay and work demands can be a challenge to agents' families. Today, at 35 years of age, and with 14 years of experience, Austin earns $90,000+ annually, and is a GS-13. A new agent coming on now would enter as a GS-5,7, or 9. According to Austin, the level is determined by both college performance, including GPA, and related experience (such as having been a local law enforcement officer, etc.).

According to Austin, the real demands of the job are relational. You are always working in some kind of team, both within the ATF, and through other agencies and departments. "I love this job. It is everything and more than what I imagined it to be." When Austin was asked what he especially liked, he said the following. "There is so much that I like, and I could ramble on and on about it. But specifically, I find the job exciting. But not the kind of excitement you see on TV. It is a real job, so don't expect to be out running around kicking in doors and arresting people. But I have worked undercover, and I have been able to bring criminals to justice. There is just something so satisfying, and even exciting about that. It's the idea of having a job to do, having the training to do it, and successfully completing it. It's the same as a doctor doing a successful surgery with his team. But the thing I really love about his job, more than any other in federal law enforcement, is the variety. We cover all firearms laws, which means dealing with convicted felons, as well as the trafficking in guns, which includes investigatory practice. In investigating gun trafficking you are trying to literally outsmart the gun-runners. This takes you to many places, and into contact with many people. Then you have arson, which is nearly always white-collar crime. Generally it is someone who is trying to deceive the insurance industry because their business is not doing well. So, you now have to use not only your training and expertise within the ATF and the state's fire marshal in order to determine what caused the fire and how it began, but you are also using bank and telephone records in order to establish patterns relevant to the fire. Then you take all this evidence and present it to the US Attorney's office and convince them that there is indeed a case. And you eventually have to convince a jury. Once this all comes together you have such a great feeling of achievement. I guess this is what I mean by excitement in my job." But it is still the variety of cases which keeps the job interesting, besides exciting. In addition to firearms and arson Austin has certifications in the handling and disposal of explosives and explosive devices. His work in this area has been as mundane as safely clearing old dynamite from some farm, to tracking children who have learned how to made bombs from the internet. In many of these cases, such as the World Trade Center bombing, and the Oklahoma City bombing, the ATF works in conjunction with still other agencies such as the FBI. But in most of these cases, according to Austin, he gets to actually run the investigations. At the time of this interview Austin was running fifteen active investigations. It is his job to evaluate the case, determine a plan, carry it out, and continuously assess the investigation for progress. According to Austin, "This kind of authority is unique to the ATF."

In addition to specific ATF functions Austin has also worked in conjunction with other federal agency details. In his years he has worked with the secret service on five different presidential campaigns, including service to Presidents Bush, Sr., Clinton, and Vice President Gore. He has worked with the State Department in service to the Prime Minister of Bahrain. His job there was basically security, making sure the official is transported safely throughout their travels while in this country. According to Austin, "You not only are working the details of security with a foreign dignitary, but you are also working with their security team. They are the experts on that particular person, and you have to figure out a way to mesh with them and their practices. Some of the details include inspecting the vehicles used, or securing restaurants and hotel rooms. And sometimes they (the dignitary) will jump out on you. You think that you are going to the Metropolitan Opera and they decide to stop for a snack. So, you have to immediately secure a new area. Communication is a high priority in such assignments." Interestingly, in the week after working with the Minister of Bahrain, Austin was assigned to the Foreign Minister of Japan, with a larger contingent of security, and different practices. Other such assignments have included the Presidents of Slovakia and Ghana.

Austin is also a member of the National Response Team. Their primary task is to respond to major fires and explosions which occur throughout the country. In this capacity Austin worked events such as the World Trade Organization (WTO) meetings in Seattle, Oklahoma City, where he investigated Timothy McVeigh's activities prior to the bombing, a fireworks factory explosion in Michigan, and many others. His work takes him all across the United States as a part of the National Response Team. According to Austin, "Most have no idea that there is such vairety in work and locale as I have experienced in the ATF. It's one of the things that keeps my work so interesting." Part of this variety is due to the relatively small size of the ATF force. Presently there are approximately 1300 special agents nationwide. Although Austin feels that there really needs to be more like 2000 special agents to adequately cover the workload. In addition there are about 800 inspectors, whose job it is to make sure a new winery, or gun shop, for example, are following all necessary steps and regulations according to law.

Austin believes that the relatively small size of ATF has actually enhanced the ability of special agents to work through and around other agencies. This skill at cooperation and coordination facilitates a high rate of success in fighting crime. According to Austin, "While it may sound like bragging, there are somewhere around 12,000 FBI agents, compared to 1300 ATF agents, but the ATF prosecutes within a couple of hundred as many as the FBI. It's my opinion that this is due precisely to the rapport the ATF has with local authorities."

It is this latter point that contributes significantly to Austin's love of what he does. The relationships he has built up over 14 years has produced not only a record of high quality work, but a kind of professional and personal stability. He recently turned down a supervisory position, in part because his priority is his young family. At the same time Austin does think about his longer term future. At age 46 he could retire with 25 years of experience. When asked what he would do if he retired then, he suggested that working in the insurance field as a consultant is kind of appealing. But, he is keeping his options open for now.

Finally, Austin has the following advice for someone interested in a career in ATF. Austin was very clear in his first piece of advice. "Regardless of what you may want to do in law enforcement, choose a major that you are going to enjoy. The four years of college are going to be the best four years of your life, and you'll want to enjoy them." Interestingly, it is not so much a matter of the particular degree that you earn which dictates your opportunities in this field. According to Austin, "If you are a good person, and have basic skills, you'll eventually get an opportunity. However, you should know that decisions you make now, not in terms of degree, but in terms of how hard you're willing to work while in college, will in the end prove most important. If you just scrape by in college, and then try to convince ATF interviewers that you are now a different person and are willing to do what is necessary to fulfill the mission of the ATF, it's not going to cut it. Perhaps even more important is how you conduct yourself as a person. It does matter whether you have a record, have used drugs, etc. You will be asked, point blank, about your personal history, and you will do so on a polygraph. It just means that you need to take care of who you are, now. You have to be trustworthy, you must be ethical. So, if you were to even sweep under the rug a less than perfect past, you will find it hard to succeed in ATF. The reason is, eventually every case relies on your believability as an expert or a witness before a judge and jury."

Austin advises to plan ahead. "In fact, if you are a sophomore or junior right now (2001), this is the perfect time to be going into federal law enforcement. There are tons of jobs, specifically because we in this country want a safe society." This does not mean that all jobs are directly open to first time applicants. According to Austin, "Get any experience you can. Do internships, take a local law enforcement position, anything that gets you in. You can always move around afterwards. A recent hire in my office started off as an investigator in the Department of Transportation, then did likewise in the Department of Labor, and finally moved laterally into ATF. Last year alone, 200 US Marshals transferred to ATF."

In conclusion, Austin says, "Be persistent, and be aggressive. Get to know people in the field, even those not specifically in the kind of position you envision. It does not matter where you start out in law enforcement, but it does matter where you end up."

21

BORDER PATROL AGENT/
U.S. MARSHALL

According to Bill Dillon, "There are some people who know, even when they are ten years old that they want to be in law enforcement. That was my brother. He knew from day one that he wanted to go into law enforcement. In my case, it never even crossed my mind, until I was about 20 years old. Until then I had no interest in it, whatsoever." By the time Bill was a junior in college other people, including his brother, began to influence his career interests. One friend, two years older than Bill, had taken a position with the ATF, and they talked off and on about the ATF as a possibility. Another family member was also in federal law enforcement, as a special agent in the state department. Bill also talked with him about possibilities. These discussions "...peaked my interest," according to Bill. "I was drawn to the freedom of movement, the possibilities, the fact that you could work in any state of the country, including overseas. At age 21 all of this was rather appealing."

Given Bill's rather uneven venture into law enforcement, it is interesting to note that his earlier intentions in college were to pursue private sector employment. He was earning a degree in economics, and thought perhaps he might someday be a banker. "But," according to Bill, "I really wasn't sure. I was so close to graduation that I just didn't want to change my major. Even as I began thinking more about law enforcement I knew that to change my major would add another year to a year and a half. I did not want to do that." It should be noted that Bill's extended family has an extensive history in law enforcement, and he did have access to plenty of advice. But he was not all that certain that other family members would necessarily be supportive of a decision to go into law enforcement.

So, Bill graduated in 1988, with an idea that he would not pursue banking, or any other career specifically related to his degree in economics. Instead he began testing for a variety of law enforcement jobs. According to Bill, "Almost every government related job begins with a testing process. Even though I did not know just where this process would take me, it was necessary to do the testing. I took the treasury enforcement test for the Bureau of Alcohol, Tobacco, and Firearms (ATF), Secret Service, and US Customs. About that same time, in early 1989, I took the Border Patrol test. I'd also applied for a few other jobs, such as with the State Department, and even jobs in the White House. But I really didn't hear anything from any of these applications or exams, for a long time. In fact, I got no feedback for two years on any of them. It was really discouraging. However, everyone I knew, who knew anything about this process, had told me that this is the way it would be. So, while I was disappointed, it wasn't something unexpected."

This meant that Bill had to do something else while he waited for his law enforcement future to begin to pan out. While in college Bill had worked for UPS for nearly three years, and he continued to do so for a short time after graduation. Rather soon he moved home, lived with his parents, and worked in a warehouse in town. He did this for about a year before taking another job, basically driving a delivery truck. According to Bill, "The whole time I knew I was close to getting a job, so it was really hard to apply myself to those jobs, knowing it wasn't something I really wanted to do, and I had something else that hopefully was about to happen." Bill was just biding his time. "I'd received my ATF test scores, and was also told that I'd passed the Border Patrol exam, but other than that I really did not hear much. Although I did hear that ATF was in a complete hiring freeze." Bill was hopeful, though the prospects were not advancing very quickly.

Eventually, in August of 1991, Bill was interviewed by the Border Patrol, and, "They told me that I was hired! They told me I was going to go to the academy, that I had a job, that I'd receive notification of where I was going, everything. I couldn't have been more excited. While I had hope for this, it was also kind of unexpected. I'd waited for so long, and now all at once it seemed to be coming together." The actual interview was rather demanding. Bill recalls it as a four hour session with two assistant chiefs and a chief of the Border Patrol. However, it was very informal. According to Bill, "They asked me questions more about myself, personally, rather than anything about my specific qualifications. They asked questions such as, could I work alone, how did I feel about working with guns, could I confront people, was I prepared to be shot at, etc.? These were not questions that I ever imagined I'd be asked in an interview with the Border Patrol." When asked about these questions, Bill explained that at that time the attrition rate for the Border Patrol was so high that the interviewers were more interested in a candidate's capacity for enduring the challenges of the work than other variables.

Bill was, as he said, "excited" about the new job. But then, according to Bill, "I went to my current job, where I was really miserable, and made the biggest mistake I could have made. I told my boss that I was probably going to be leaving. The Border Patrol people had led me to believe that I'd be assigned within weeks. But I did not hear from them again for five months. Well, the guys at work were really riding me by then. I was hearing things like, 'What's happening with this great government job you're supposed to be getting?' Then, one day I get home from work and I have this certified letter, and it said that I was being sent to Imperial Beach, California, and I had just two weeks to get there!" While Bill was glad to be getting on with his career in law enforcement, he understood that such an assignment could be very hard on family life. While he was not married at that time, he was involved in a serious relationship. Bill feels that he was very fortunate to have been assigned to the San Diego area, as it proved less difficult on his other relationships.

In April of 1992 Bill reported for Border Patrol duty to the San Diego Sector Headquarters in southern California. He was there for three days of processing. Bill's first impressions are not so encouraging. As Bill tells it, "My cousin drove me out to the Border Patrol station that first day. It sits about two miles north of the border. The roads are in a desert like area, and I'm seeing aliens, in groups of ten or twenty, running up and down the road. It seemed so completely out of control. You see, I'd never even been in California before that. I was in total shock. The next day the other recruits and I show up at the station, and here I see guys wearing all kinds of things. I see guys dressed in suits with Ray-Ban glasses, while other guys were dressed in shorts and tank tops. None of us knew what to expect. So, they sat us down and belittled us for three days, telling us that we probably won't make it, and that at least half of us will wash out. It was just kind of like boot camp." After three days Bill was then sent out to Georgia for the Border Patrol academy. It lasted 19 weeks. According to Bill, "It was more of the same. The first day they had us in uniforms, marching, made everybody go get haircuts. The funny thing is, this is the same academy where all other federal agents, except the FBI, goes for training. It's really like a college campus, but agents from the other agencies are wearing regular clothes. But the Border Patrol is in uniform, and we have to march wherever we go. So, here I am, in these hot green uniforms, in Georgia, in summer, and I'm just miserable." It seems that the Border Patrol has a particular image to uphold, that of being paramilitary. And they begin ingraining that in recruits while in the academy.

There are several reasons that the Border Patrol academy was 19 weeks, longer than most other federal agency academies. It is a difficult academy, in part because the work of the Border Patrol is also difficult. If agents are not prepared enough, then they will simply not make it in the field. According to Bill, "There are two really tough things about the academy. The first is immigration law, which is horribly complex. On the first immigration law exam I took, over 60% of the class failed. And, if you failed two exams in a row, you were gone. So, the stress level is high in that regard. The other thing was Spanish. That was just terrible. You've got 19 weeks to learn Spanish, you're in class three hours every day. And you had PT (physical training) every day. You just ran and ran." Out of 48 in Bill's academy class, 26 actually made it through to graduation. Bill recalled that the first day of the academy five recruits quit. Besides immigration law, there was also an overview of statutory law, just as an introduction to gun and narcotics laws, etc. This allowed the new agents to be cross-designated in all these fields, allowing them to make arrests as they needed. They also shot at the range, almost everyday. According to Bill, "…that was a really humbling experience. You see, I grew up around guns, hunting and all that, and I thought I'd just be a natural, and I just couldn't shoot at all. It was embarrassing. I had to go to remedial training, as did a lot of people. Looking at it from now, it's kind of funny, though it wasn't so funny then."

Once the academy is completed, new agents are then sent back to their station; in Bill's case, California. But the new agents are still in training status. The job title is Border Patrol Agent. While still in training new agents are assigned to a training unit, which is all the academy classmates assigned to that station. Together, new agents work with a training officer, an agent with three to five years experience. Training in the field goes on for another six months. After six months in the field new agents must take another law and Spanish exam. According to Bill, "The Spanish test is taken orally in front of thee of the assistant chiefs in the sector. You must ask them twenty questions in Spanish, which are in writing in English before you. They then answer back in Spanish, and you have to write down what they tell you." If new agents pass this round of exams there is another round in four more months. This ten-month exam must be passed in order to keep your job. Passing this last exam, the new agent is now fully a part of the Border Patrol. In light of this experience, Bill now says, "While in college I just did not have any idea how important speaking another language would eventually be to me. It would have been really helpful to have had at least a couple of courses while in school. I mean, I had one year of high school Spanish, and at the academy we were past that in the first day. They just move so fast." Now nine years later, I asked how good Bill was in Spanish. According to Bill, while he has since moved on to the US Marshal's service, he nonetheless uses his Spanish almost weekly. He rates his Spanish as, "Pretty good. It's nice to have."

When Bill finally finished his field training, nearly a year after the days at the academy, he was now ready to do the job of a Border Patrol Agent. In Bill's opinion, the sector he was in, was in "complete chaos." The sector was short on manpower, the vehicles were not functioning. Washington would send maybe twenty new sedans per year to the sector. But everything Bill's sector did was in the mountains, river beds, etc., and there was just no use for a sedan. "For some reason, we just could not get it through their (Washington's) head that what we needed were four-wheel drive vehicles. You were just constantly on foot, having to park your car and walk into the river valleys and lay up on trails. I worked midnight's for three years. On a given night, our station, which would be 25 agents, or less, would catch anywhere from 300 to 1000 people trying to cross the border. All of them then had to be processed through the station. Sometimes one or more of them had to be passed on for criminal procedures. It was just really overwhelming. We were lucky of we caught half of those crossing the border. And that was just the foot traffic. Every once in a while a very large group would come across the border, but interestingly these would not be Mexicans, they would be Chinese, smuggled in by armed Mexicans. And of course, we had no Chinese speaking agents. It was really kind of pathetic. There were also vans and trucks, loaded with aliens, which would run the port, and then there would be a vehicle pursuit. This was a really dangerous situation, and it happened almost every three hours! One tactic of the smugglers in a pursuit was to push people out of the vehicle, and into the other traffic, thereby causing a pile-up on the road and giving the smugglers a chance to get away. Like I said, it was really pathetic. It was also unbelievable."

When Bill got to his first station assignment, nearly 90% of the agents had been there five years or less. According to Bill, "The morale was very gung-ho and positive. After about three years or so, agents became bitter, fed-up, and so on. A lot of the agents just didn't want to do anything anymore. This became a real problem among the agents, as there always seemed to be a separation between the guys ready to do the job, and those who'd given up." However, in 1995 the budget for Border Patrols was nearly tripled, and new equipment flooded in , in particular four-wheel drive vehicles, and manpower was significantly increased. According to Bill, "Operation Gatekeeper began at that time. Everyone was moved right up to the line, and you sat there all night. It really worked in our sector. But it moved the flow of aliens across the border way to the east, almost to Arizona."

When Bill started as a new Border Patrol Agent in 1992, he was paid just over $20,000 per year. As soon as he completed the academy his pay increased by 25% as a kind of mandatory overtime. There were also bonuses for night and weekend work. So, in Bill's first full year, he made just over $40,000. After about five years as a Border Patrol agent, Bill was making in the low $50,000's. But, Bill's last few months there he was working 14 to 15 hours a day. "That," according to Bill, "was not working well with my family. In addition, my time on a customs task force was coming to an end, and I knew that I was returning to line duty, and that just no longer appealed to me. We no longer worked cases, we were just sitting at a point on the border, trying to hold back traffic. The fun was over. My opinion is that it's great for a while, but it's really a young man's job. There's so much physical activity, climbing around the mountains and actually chasing people. It's just really hard on the body."

Eventually Bill began looking for a kind of criminal investigator's job. According to Bill, "My scope at that time was ATF, DEA, and the US Marshal's service. I applied with all of them. But only DEA and the Marshal's service were hiring." Bill ended up interviewing with both agencies, and had decided to go with which ever agency offered a position. The process is much like all other federal law enforcement jobs. There is a rather lengthy application, and then an exam. Then, it is simply waiting for the exam scores. This all takes approximately six months. Based on score, applicants are then called for interviews. According to Bill, "One guy in my office was hired before me, and he was sent to the Midwest. He and I were also classmates at the academy. About six months later I interviewed and was told that I'd be offered a position. Originally I was to be sent to either San Francisco or Los Angeles, but I really wanted to return to the Midwest. So, I called my friend and spoke to the Marshal too, and they helped to arrange for me to be hired with them." That was in November of 1996. "And, I'm back in the academy again. The exact same place. But the difference from marching around with the Border Patrol recruits was huge. There was no marching, no saluting, no inspections. Also, I'd been through most of the classes, and there was a lot of repetition. I knew what to expect. It was actually reasonably fun the second time around. I was already in shape from my last job, there was no Spanish, and it was only 16 weeks instead of 19."

Now Bill is in a new kind of law enforcement environment. Given that he was still in the federal system all of his pay related factors just lateraled over to his new position; including grade, pay scale, vacation accrued, etc. Right now, as a GS-12, Bill is making in the range of $60,000-$70,000 per year. His new job title is Deputy US Marshal. But his government classification is Criminal Investigator 1811. According to Bill, the financial benefits of his new position are outstanding. But perhaps more significantly, the job is totally different from the Border Patrol.

According to Bill, the US Marshal's service is in charge of three different areas. One is pre-trial prisoner custody for federal prisoners. For example, if the DEA makes an arrest, they would transfer the prisoner to the US Marshal's service for custody. It is their job to find a jail to house the prisoner, and then to go with the prisoner to all hearings or trials leading up to the conclusion of the case. The Marshal's service is also charged with the judge's security. Finally, they work warrants. They serve all federal warrants and make the arrests. If there is an escape from a prison, the Marshal's service is responsible for organizing the recapture. This is the one area, among all the things the Marshal's service does, according to Bill, that they are really good at doing. "It is amazing," according to Bill, "how good the Service can be a tracking fugitives, whether it is studying phone or credit card bills, or interviewing friends and family. They know how to track."

The job skill set for being a US Marshal includes the following. According to Bill, "Communication is huge, especially during an investigation. Let's say you are trying to find someone who is a fugitive. Nine times out of ten you'll find this person by means of an interview. You see, we deal with all these fugitives, and there are similarities among the cases. Nearly every fugitive is in contact with someone in their family, or a girlfriend. And if you can find out who that girlfriend is, you'll almost always find that person. Most people have no idea how to do interviews, at least those which produce something. I know that I thought I had good interview skills when I got here, but I found out that I didn't. I've taken a lot of training over the years to improve them." As examples, Bill related some of the assumptions he makes heading into an interview. Perhaps the most important is knowing that people want to talk. Many times interviewers want to "brow beat" someone, but for Bill that never really works. Rather he tries to make the interview subject comfortable about talking. In this way, according to Bill, they will almost always tell you what you want to know.

One matter of significance is the need for continued development of one's skills as a law enforcement officer. According to Bill, he suggests that he is always looking for opportunities for additional training. As in the question of interviewing, mentioned just above, there are actually companies which conduct special seminars in interviewing and interrogation. The Marshal's service has a training budget, and Bill is constantly looking for professional development opportunities. One simple reason for such is that the nature of criminal activity continues to evolve. You must know more than you do now in order to keep up. One recent training served as preparation for a task force on clandestine methamphetamine labs. Without appropriate training, according to Bill, you could easily and simply inhale something that could kill you.

The best part of Bill's position in the Marshal's service is the investigation itself. According to Bill, "In any investigation you have to create the process you will use. It's totally yours. If it's good, you'll produce a good result. You are the one who has to make things happen. As a result, it is important to be self motivated." Part of this work is coordinating with other agencies. However, according to Bill, there are agency rivalries. Because of this, your communication skills, which are so important for circumstances such as interviews, are also important in overcoming agency "turf." And, sometimes local law enforcement officials just do not like federal agents coming into their county. The kinds of things we routinely see in the media about opposition to all things government, do carry over to federal law enforcement, and the ability of some Deputy US Marshal to do his or her job.

At age 35 Bill is considering his options. He is at a point where he will most likely be moving into different roles. One is more supervisory at the district level. Another is the witness security program, which falls under the Marshal's service. There are other investigative positions. Bill has interest in investigating organized crime. On the other hand, Bill could just stay right where he is. But in all these Bill sees opportunities. The question you might be asking yourself right now is, what are my opportunities? Perhaps more importantly, what must be done to make those opportunities? According to Bill, "If you really knew that going into something like the US Marshal's service was something you wanted to do, then I'd take as much English composition as I could, in order to make my writing skills as best they could be. You just have to be able to write a report. It is so important. If you can't, then you often cannot make your case. You also need those skills in order to cover yourself. Writing skills are definitely number one to me. The ability to speak another language is really nice, especially when it comes time to be hired. It is just so competitive getting into these jobs, that to be able to say that you also speak Spanish, or even better now, an eastern European language, just gives you the necessary edge to get the job. Stay in shape. You don't want to be worrying about weight when you need to be worrying about a language or the law. Also, many students think that what they want is a criminal justice degree. I just don't think that it is all that important. I work with guys from all kinds of majors, and they are all glad that they did something else. Study something that you are really interested in. The criminal justice major provides some information, but it will be your ability to stay current with the job, not what you already know that will, more than anything else, determine your future. The academy does what most people think the criminal justice degree will do. Remember, it is competitive. So, add that extra element to your education, and do something really interesting. It will make you a more interesting person."

22

DRUG ENFORCEMENT ADMINISTRATION

George Iozzo, 34, is a Special Agent for the Drug Enforcement Administration (DEA), and has been since early 1997. In general George is a criminal investigator. According to George, "Our mission is targeting major organizations trafficking in controlled substances. Basically I make my own cases, working with state and local police officers, United States attorneys and other federal agencies. We are really trying to search out and stop the big players, not necessarily the users or the street corner dealer. It's not to say that these other parts aren't important, but the DEA's mission has a different focus."

According to George, his educational path is rather unique. In the social sciences we would say that his pathway was not linear. It "zigged and zagged" across different fields and institutions. "I didn't grow up with the idea that I'd be a police officer. In fact, I had a scholarship to study dentistry. However after a couple of months I figured that I was a sharp enough guy that I didn't need a college education, and I quit. About a half a year later I decided that quitting wasn't the wisest thing I'd ever done, so I enrolled in a community college, studying psychology and working two jobs. In about a year and a half I was offered a scholarship to another university. It was then that I met my counselor, a retired probation officer and head of the criminal justice department. However, my interests were still psychology and a developing interest in math. I thought I was maybe going to head into psychiatry. But in my conversations with Jack (George's advisor), and hearing his story and career path, I began to develop a stronger interest in criminal justice, and started taking more coursework in that area."

It is often the case that the interests of an undergraduate are shaped by the opportunities presented through some faculty member, who may become a kind of mentor. This is not to say that the "shaping" is a fully intentional kind of function, whereby a student is simply molded into some form, regardless of personal interests. Rather, many such relationships evolve around opportunities to experience, either directly or via a faculty member's story, career paths not previously seen or understood. For example, in organized and white collar crime, much of the criminal activity is conducted via financial institutions. Thus, an understanding of accounting and computers is essential to any investigation of such crime. Most students with interests in criminal justice do not have such ideas guiding them. In another case a student of mine undertook an internship with a small town police department. In the course of the internship she was offered training in as a dispatcher, and later in 911 emergency calls. She eventually studied to be an EMT (emergency medical technician) as a direct result of the kinds of calls she was handling, and a developing interest in what was happening in that field. The obvious lesson here is, be open to ideas and pathways not already in your sites. In a very real sense, there is much more that you do not yet know about the field and the opportunities it holds, than what you do know. This is the very purpose of your education, and it was certainly George's experience.

In George's experience thus far he had learned that as an employee he needed constant challenge. While he seemed to do well at various jobs, he also felt that he was not likely to keep a job long before moving on. What he found in criminal justice was just the kind of stimulating variety he needed, and which seemed capable of holding his interest. "While I was listening to Jack, I knew that work in criminal justice was a daily challenge. Just what I needed and wanted. Jack's life and career demonstrated this quality, and I became more and more drawn to it." While George was still an undergraduate the Dallas, Texas police department was conducting a nation-wide recruiting tour for new officers. According to George, "They were trying to break their image of being a *good ol' boy* police department. In 1989 and 1990 their search took them to nearly every state. They were looking for recruits with a four year degree, with some different kinds of experience, and a better understanding of people." So, when they came to his school, George tested and interviewed with the recruiters. George felt that, "They were looking for people who could reason, who would not make judgments based on bias. At that time there was a lot of racial and ethnic tension, within the community of Dallas, between the community and the police department, and within the department as well. So, they seemed to be looking for new officers who could work well with people from a variety of backgrounds. And, as an undergrad I'd had experience with students from all around the country, and even the world, including Asians, Hispanics, African Americans, etc. It had been a normal part of my education to interact in a diverse environment, and that seemed to be what the recruiters were looking for in new officers."

Given the times, George believes that it was assumed that if you were going into law enforcement, you would naturally study criminal justice as a prerequisite. However, George now says, "If there was anything I could have changed about my undergraduate education, it would be that I would not have settled for a criminal justice degree. I'd had designs on double majoring in math, but I ended up a half semester short." George's reasoning is, taking a wider variety of courses, in the sciences, arts, even theology, make you a much more well rounded person. And, it is your ability to relate to an ever widening array of people, under an equally widening array of circumstances, which will determine your success as a law enforcement officer. It is not that the criminal justice degree isn't useful, but it is, in George's words, "limited." George now feels that a degree in something else, either in addition to criminal justice, or instead of criminal justice, actually makes one "more attractive." He is convinced of this now after having worked as a law enforcement officer at the village, large city, state and now federal levels. It also interesting to know that prior to the interviews with the Dallas recruiters, George had already take the LSAT (admissions exam for law school) and was accepted, and had also worked with a Marine Corps recruiter for Officer Candidate School. His intent was to eventually go into a JAG (Judge

Advocate General) program.

The point must be made here that George's whole educational experience has taught him the value of diversity of experience, as well as the wisdom of creating multiple educational and career opportunities. Too many times students assume the linear program of degree and career mentioned above. In George's case, in spite of some less than wise decisions, he nonetheless was able to recover, precisely because he had a variety of interests, and had created a variety of opportunities. According to George, "Actually I was signed, sealed, and delivered to the JAG program. But, the summer courses of study I would have begun were canceled. So, I had to decide whether I would wait to see if a class made for September, or I would take the job offered in Dallas. I decided to take the job in Dallas. Good or bad, that decision totally changed my life, due to the way things have since worked out. In fact, it was a very good decision. While I wouldn't change anything, I do sometimes wonder how things would have been different given different circumstances and decisions." To conclude this point, having options is always an advantage. You may have some difficult decisions to make, but having them to make is far superior than having your one objective not develop. Here is an example which might give you pause as you consider this particular lesson. Recently a student from another department came to my office seeking advice about a new major, or perhaps a second major. As I inquired further I found that the student had volunteered in working with wayward youth, and had hopes of doing likewise after college. After we had explored the options of my department, which offered career tracks in sociology, social work, and justice studies, I asked the student the following question. "When you are 50 years old, do you still see yourself working with wayward youth?" In other words, did this student see themselves dedicating nearly 30 years to this cause. Perhaps. But more likely he will be pursuing other kinds of career paths, or at least other dimensions of service to young people having a hard time with life. So, ask yourself, given your present interests, do you see yourself dedicated to this one career for your entire work life?

So, in 1990 George Iozzo took the offer from Dallas to become a police officer, a regular patrolman. George admits to the draw of the financial security the new position offered. "I was being offered a full time job, with benefits, vacation and $26,000 a year in salary! I had worked my way all through college, and it seemed as if now all that work had finally paid off." However, even though George had attended college in the Chicago area, his life before that was primarily rural. As he says, "I hadn't really been exposed to a lot. I knew a couple of kids who had smoked marijuana, but that was about it. I'd never even really seen the inner city. And here I am, 21, fresh out of college, little in the way of experience, and I'm working the projects of Dallas. My first call is a dead body. A kid had been shot 11 times at close range with a nine millimeter. I'd seen stories of such on TV, but seeing it for real was very difficult. In fact, it was kind of hard to actually believe how brutally people could treat each other." George admits to having significant second thoughts about his choice. The money was good, but the work was hard to tolerate. He even had thoughts of returning to law school.

Before actually hitting the streets, George attended the Dallas Police Academy for 26 weeks. According to George, "It was fun, I was energetic, I liked the opportunity to prove myself." A day in the academy began at 6:00 AM, though George did not have to live at the academy. "They

97

taught us everything, including Spanish; or at least law enforcement Spanish. The academy was a challenge, and I did well." George graduated near the top of the class. But the work he then went on to do somehow fell short of the kind of stimulation he had hoped would be a part of the work. Yes, there was variety in the details day to day, but at the same time everyday was the same. According to George, "You were just in a kind of zone while at work. I'd still get the adrenaline rush when we'd get a call, but the handling of calls was essentially the same, from what you did at the scene, to the paperwork you did to follow up. It was a good job, but not what I'd really hoped for in terms of a mental challenge." This does not mean, however, that George was not doing his best, nor that he was simply going through the motions. He continued to observe the work of the police, and noticed a number of attributes which facilitated good police work. The first skill, or attribute George mentioned was patience. "If you had a level of patience, and are willing to listen, then you can defuse nearly any situation. In my eleven years of law enforcement I've been in a physical fight only twice. I have learned how to calm situations by not shouting, not trying to intimidate, and by listening to those involved. I was even thanked once by a minority suspect who was surprised that I did not attempt to beat him. He was grateful that I'd treated him with respect. You need to understand, that in order to be a good police officer, you need to be able to see things objectively, because not everything is what if may seem to be at first."

George stayed with Dallas police for about two years, when he heard of an opening in the DEA. According to George, notice of the position came via a DEA vacancy announcement. These are broadcast widely throughout law enforcement. Further, his old college advisor, Jack, was looking out for him. So George applied to DEA. But it must be understood that as in all lives, there are multiple factors which influence our decisions. Just as George had Jack continuing to advise and open doors, George also had family concerns. It became evident that for the sake of his family, a return to the Midwest was necessary. While the money was good, the stress of a new marriage, child, job, and location, required some rethinking of priorities. However, the DEA did not hire at that time, and George was in a kind of career and family limbo. He considered returning to law school, but eventually took a position as a police officer in a small but affluent town, quite different from Dallas. This was 1992. Interestingly, according to George, "In the interview there was some apprehension expressed about hiring me, specifically because I was now from a large city. They were worried that having been a Dallas police officer I would not transfer well to the small town. Here I was already feeling the effects of the stereotype I'd heard about when I was recruited to Dallas in the first place. But it is a different place, it's night and day difference. Calls we wouldn't even respond to in Dallas were common place there. In Dallas we'd get a call for 'shots fired.' But we weren't even going to investigate that. How were we going to track down the origin of some random shots in that city, especially when five other more pressing calls were awaiting our attention. Then I find myself back in the Midwest, and I get a call to go to an address and turn on the sprinkler! I guess I did have a little big city arrogance, and I replied that that didn't require my attention. My Sargent came over the radio and told me that I would respond to the call, and that afterwards I would report to him at the station. It was just a whole different kind of community."

As a function of his new job, he was required to attend he state police academy for ten weeks.

98

According to George, "I'm a little older, I've already been through an academy, and I have to live there for the duration. I consider myself experienced and educated, yet this is more of the old military style academy. I guess I did have a kind of attitude about things, in part because I was experienced, and I wasn't a chump. But they were treating me that way, and I was very close to walking out. If I'd wanted that kind of treatment, then I'd have gone into the military. But I did stick it out, though a number of others in my class did quit. I just wanted to get my training and get back to my job." George did later explain that he had issues with the philosophy of the state police academy, especially given the kind of public service orientation law enforcement officers would eventually have to deliver. To be treated as a rookie military recruit, and then to expect them to behave in a quite different way towards the public, just seemed too contradictory to George. Nonetheless, for the next five years George worked as a small town police officer.

In 1994 (three years before he was eventually hired by the DEA) George reapplied to the DEA. According to George, the federal law enforcement hiring system is incredibly slow. It often takes multiple submissions of application materials. And, due to the high rate of transfers and other mobility in the system, the process often breaks down. So, the officials responsible for background checks get transferred, and your application simply stops. According to George, you must be very persistent and exercise a lot of patience in the federal process. Be prepared for a longer, rather than a shorter process. So, what eventually made the difference in George being hired by the DEA? According to George, it really was not a function of his contacts. Yes, people like his old advisor, Jack, provided strong references, but the length of the process spoke against contacts making the difference. George feels it was a combination of his level of education, and excellent work recommendations. "In each case, when my previous employers were interviewed, they all said they would hire me again if given the opportunity."

A reasonable question, in light of the protracted application process, is what does DEA look for in a candidate? According to George, "I think DEA, or any of your criminal investigation organizations, are looking for a little more than most police departments. This is no slight towards the local police. The thing is, you have to hire people who are self-starters, who will do a job with minimal supervision. You need people who are self-confident, and who are comfortable with all kinds of people. On any given day I can go from interviewing a guy with an eighth grade education, to sitting in front of a judge. The DEA simply needs people who can bridge the gap. Communication is critical, and anything in your background that demonstrates that, be it education or experience, is a plus."

George was hired in 1997, and the first thing done, after getting all his paperwork in order through the office that hired him, is another academy, "My third one!" jokes George. "I'm order still, and now I have to do another 16 week academy. The style is still a bit military, though not harsh. They want a level of formality and respect that some of the other federal agencies may not promote. Included is more physical training, more running, and more intensity." So, what is the objective of the academy? According to George, "There is a class for *everything*. For example, they'll teach you Title 21, and everything related to the drug code. They also teach you about race relations, dealing with the handicapped, relating to people from diverse ethnic backgrounds, and different religious traditions. However," George believes, "if you don't already have some notion of these realities before you go to the academy, then you're not going to get it in some class, or not enough to really change someone." Some of the other course details include handling a variety of firearms, doing raids, conducting surveillance, identifying different types of drugs, etc. In George's opinion, "They do teach you a lot of good and useful things. But it is really hard, and some just do not complete the course. Occasionally, some just can't shoot, while others find out that this isn't what they wanted or expected."

Now George is graduated from the academy. Within four weeks a list of agency vacancies is distributed to the members of the class. According to George, "At least theoretically, if all members of the class agreed on where they wanted to go, then everyone would have their first choice and could work where they wanted. That, of course, is not likely. There are always some places no one wants to go. However, there is a policy that you cannot go back to the office where you were hired. If you were hired in Chicago, you cannot go back to Chicago. But I was fortunate that a slot was available at least in the vicinity of my first choice, so I was within driving distance of my daughter. I had already decided that if the job was too far away from my daughter, I'd quit. It was just not worth sacrificing the relationship. It was simply the case that my peers respected my desire to be nearer my daughter, and I was given my first choice. You literally sit there, in a room together, and decide among yourselves where you'll go. Like I said, I was very fortunate."

Starting pay for a DEA agent is a function of previous experience and government scale. A new agent with no experience starts at a GS-7, while one with experience in law enforcement starts at a GS-9. In your next year you move to either a GS-9 or 11, and in the next year a 12 for those at 11. That first year in DEA, according to George, "...is kind of a kicker. Most new agents, given that over 50% of them come from some other law enforcement job, actually take a pay cut. Salary is in the neighborhood of $30,000 plus benefits." George is now a GS-12, step 2, and is earning about $60,000. The more significant salary jump occurs at the GS-13 level.

George is now a new DEA agent, with an assignment to his first choice position. Unfortunately, according to George, "I had real bad first impressions. I'm told to report to the Division office, and I do. But they do not seem to know that I'm coming, and I don't know anyone there! After several hours I'm called and told to report to a Resident office in another part of the area. There I meet a 25 year veteran of several agencies, an intelligent man, an articulate man, a man I learned later had earned a masters degree and spoke fluent Russian. My first impression was changing for the better." In fact, George was very impressed with the caliber of his new colleague, and in particular his style of management. "While he had outstanding experience, and had done nearly everything, he did not try to overmanage my work. He suggested alternatives, but allowed me to do my job." In this regard George believes that some prior law enforcement work is an advantage, though not absolutely necessary. The advantage is that the work is not wholly new, all at once. You already have some groundwork covered, such as local policing practices, etc. It's just one less stress factor. However, according to George, the real stress of the DEA is knowing that much of the work is ongoing. In George's experience, as a police officer when your shift is over, so is the job, until the next shift. As a DEA officer, it just does not stop. It takes a while to adjust to the pace and prevalence of the work. Plus, there is much more paperwork.

The first weeks a new DEA agent is trained by a field agent. This essentially means that you are learning by doing along with a veteran. Among other things it means meeting new people, other law enforcement officers from a variety of local, state, and federal agencies, and simply trying to figure out just how to fit into to this new context. George considers these other law enforcement officers, "...the real police officers. The ones who serve as a sheriff's deputy or a police officer in a small town. Without their eyes and ears there is simply no way to be successful in the job. So, everything depends on the kinds of relationships you are able to build. Quite simply, we don't have the manpower, or the knowledge, to replicate what local officers can provide."

Cases are organized by the DEA agent, though the cases can develop in a number of different ways. Sometimes it is a matter of the agent "finding" the case on their own, but many times cases are referred by other law enforcement officers or agencies. In one example George was called by a local police department about a person from their town who had been stopped out of state in relationship to possession of methamphetamine. As it was, the police who made the stop in the other state had information that these suspects cold produce more of the "meth." Once this came to the attention of George steps taken were to bring this case into the federal system. If prosecuted in another state for the simple drug violation, the suspects would be convicted only under state law, and would serve relatively little time. But, if the suspects could be shown to be part of a larger conspiracy which transcended state lines, then federal law applies, and the corresponding prison sentences are much stiffer. So, it is a matter of coordinating with other agencies and departments to make the most appropriate charge, and to do the most damage to the organizations trafficking in controlled substances. Making a case, such as this, is always a matter of negotiation and management of essential relationships. Sometimes citizens just call in with concerns about neighbors or others in their community. You of course must be careful to respect the rights of all involved, but that again goes to your capacity to manage essential relationships. If you had developed good local law enforcement relationships in a particular town, and you received a citizen call from that town, you then could at least check it out via your contacts first, before perhaps blundering into what may be just "bad blood" among neighbors. According to George, "I just couldn't do my job without these relationships."

Besides relationships George suggests that the work of a DEA agent requires adaptability, innovation, and an ability to think quickly on your feet. A good bit of this comes from experience. But without such skills, just like the relationships, you are not likely to get the job done. It is important to note that the target, organizations given to trafficking in drugs, are always a moving target. If you are not flexible, the target will simply move out of your radar. According to George, "Just expect your initial plan to change, at any time. But nothing substitutes for hard work."

George now has been a DEA agent for four years. His 11 years in law enforcement have been marked by relatively brief tenures; witness the three different academies he has attended. George is also very committed to family, especially his daughter. In addition, George has begun to do more in the way of teaching DEA-related courses. He himself has taken a variety of such courses, ranging from Clandestine Methamphetamine Training, to Techniques in Interviewing

101

and Interrogation, to Administration of Asset Forfeiture. But teaching is becoming more and more attractive. When this interest is combined with his perspective on children, George has begun to consider that his best option for impacting the most people may be in the teaching of children in some capacity, perhaps in school. The point is, "We cannot fully kick the drug problem. We can keep some of it off the street, and maybe even save someone's life in the process. But I'm just not sure where the best opportunity for positively impacting others will lead me."

Among other things, George has learned what it takes to be a DEA agent. So, what advice might he have for someone following in his footsteps? His first advice is to learn another language. Any language, as long as you enjoy it. The most marketable now is Spanish, but the diversity of our United States makes nearly any language of value to law enforcement generally, and the DEA specifically. Interestingly, while George does not discourage students from getting degrees in criminal justice, he suggests that you are much better off getting degrees in areas that are interesting to you. Then find out how those might apply to careers in law enforcement, such as the DEA. Further, it is quite possible that once in the field you may find it is taking you places you do not want to go. Or, you may just tire of the career. What then?

Ultimately, George advises to know clearly and act accordingly to what you really value. One of George's sources of pride as a DEA agent is the role model he provides for his daughter. It is not the job you should be pursuing, it is the values you evidence that are finally most important.

23

MITIGATION/
PRIVATE INVESTIGATION

In the early 1970's Nicole Long was majoring in psychology, minoring in sociology, and preparing to be a social studies teacher. She completed her degree in three years, graduating in 1974. Her classes in sociology, according to Nicole, were mostly just fun, although she also did rather well in them. Soon after graduation Nicole signed on to serve as a VISTA volunteer in Louisiana. According to Nicole, "The first program I was sent to was some Nuns in Louisiana. They were bringing in these VISTA volunteers to bring about social change under the guise of social service. So, we drove around and tried to hook people up with food stamps, and otherwise bring social services to them. While doing this we also developed relationships with the people we served, and our intent was to eventually mobilize them for social change. You see, at that time, and in that part of the south, there were circumstances which still reflected slavery. One example of this was the old system of the company store, which literally trapped people economically. And the schools were so inadequate that children attending there simply could not escape. There was even a language spoken in this one plantation area which was a kind of Cajun, kind of Creole, kind of English. But hardly anyone outside that plantation could even understand it. The people living there were trapped by that language as well. There were all kinds of invisible bars which kept people on the plantations, and kept those systems in place. There was a need for change. So, that is where I was, at 21 years of age, and it was a really impactful experience. In fact, it has impacted everything about me since then."

After about three years Nicole decided to return to school for a masters degree in counseling, but there was a rather interesting twist. "When I wrote to my major advisor, in psychology, I found out he didn't even remember me! Here I'd earned a 4.0 in psychology just three years before, and he doesn't even remember me. I'd also written to my advisor in sociology, and even though I'd only minored in that, he remembered who I was. Sometimes small things like this can create significant turning points in one's life." While studying for that degree, which she earned in 1978, Nicole also went to work in a variety of social service organizations. "I was really working with a number of special projects, working with kids, working with low income families, basically working with special needs populations. Actually I was part of that population, being a low income woman with kids. For example, we organized child care co-ops so we could go to school. In fact, in three of the places I've lived I've organized child care co-ops because child care has been such a significant expense for me. Really, my whole life has been given to private, non-profit, grass-roots organizations. In many ways I started out as an activist, and I still am."

By 1982 Nicole left the far west and came back east. Actually she traveled for about six months, visiting friends, and thinking more about furthering her education beyond the masters. Among other things she was considering fields such as human developmental counseling and counseling in education. "While I was considering my options, I should say that I never, ever, ever considered sociology." This is rather interesting because Nicole's activist bent was a natural fit for sociology, and that she had minored in sociology as an undergraduate. It becomes even more interesting when Nicole eventually earns a Ph.D. in sociology. How did this happen? According to Nicole, "I was accepted to graduate school twice, 1983 and 1984, in human developmental counseling. But I was not offered any funding, and that was essential to me being able to attend. However, on a visit to mother's I passed by a university I'd not really considered, and simply decided to submit an application, just on a chance. Not only was I accepted, but I was also funded! It had just become so clear to me that in my situation I was not going to be able to both work and go to school. It was just impossible. So, in three months I was off to a Ph.D. program in sociology." When Nicole was asked, 'Why sociology?', she replied, "It was already evident that I needed a different situation, as I wasn't getting anywhere in the programs to which I had already applied. While I had a major in psychology and could have gone on in that, I just didn't like it from a political perspective. I felt that it was oriented to blaming the victim. It tried to individualize problems that were just clearly not individual. In one sense, I was being driven towards sociology by my own experiences. I also had a particular experience while working with a domestic violence program. It seemed that the domestic violence counseling centers were operating on three basic facts: domestic violence was contagious and you were going to infect the next generation, it was untreatable, and that it would escalate. Therefore, the only real guidance for a woman calling the hotline was that you must go, there is no hope. You must get out of that relationship. When I understood this I found that I tended to agree with the notion that it was generational, and that it tended to escalate, but I did have a problem with the notion that it was untreatable, and that there was only one option, get out. So, I went to the source of these facts, and the data which supported them, and found that it was sociological research which had produced them. In a sense, in my work I rediscovered sociology. When this was combined with the other factors in my life, it seemed that I just kind of landed in sociology."

Ann eventually did her doctoral dissertation back in the context of domestic violence. One of the groundbreaking insights Nicole brought to the study of domestic violence was that "crime within the family was indeed crime." What Nicole did was to use criminological theory--social bonding theory-- to study what heretofore had been seen more as dysfunction. It is widely accepted today that certain family dysfunction's, such as child sexual abuse, is actually a crime. But fifteen to twenty years ago that was not the case. This made Nicole's research very controversial. "Given that I was really that activist at heart that I mentioned before, I was oriented towards solutions to the problems I was confronting. Sociology seemed to have answers that I just wasn't going to get from counseling or psychology. What's missing is the vision. There's just not much hope for answers. Nicole graduated with her Ph.D. in sociology in 1989.

In Nicole's last year of graduate studies, while she was writing her dissertation based on the domestic violence research cited above, she was on a university fellowship. This allowed her to write full time, and in her first semester she essentially finished the work. She credits her dissertation director for creating the kind of atmosphere and demand to get the job done, that she was able to complete the work so quickly. It also fit with Nicole's emerging interests in applied sociology. Though not identified as such, Nicole was still interested in social change, and in the applications of sociological theory to the problems at hand. The dissertation was just another problem to be solved. As a result of her efficiency, Nicole took a temporary teaching position at a local university for the spring semester. And then, a chance meeting changed the course of Nicole's life and career. According to Nicole, "It was at that time that I met a death penalty attorney who recruited me into the field that I'm still in. While we'd met through mutual friends, he basically came over to my house to look at an upstairs apartment. While he was there he noticed some kind of a badge from a criminology conference I'd attended stuck on a bulletin board, and he asked about it." Eventually, this attorney asked Nicole if she would do some interviews for him. The story was that he was the attorney for a defendant in a death penalty case. Once convicted the defendant then had to appear for a sentencing hearing. Essentially, the attorney wanted testimony from his client's family members as information to be presented at the sentencing hearing. Nicole, in interviewing them, found that the family members did not really want to testify. So, at the sentencing hearing, Nicole became the *de facto* expert witness regarding this defendant and his family circumstances and upbringing. However, as Nicole recalls, "In my very first case of this kind, the jury recommended the death penalty." It was a rather inauspicious start to a new career.

While Nicole's education and work careers had coalesced to a point where she would be doing cutting edge work in criminal justice, she had also stumbled onto a pathway that would lead her into all kinds of uncharted waters. As Nicole thinks back over that first assignment by the attorney, she concludes that there was just so much that she did not know, nor even know to ask. Nicole was operating in a vacuum. As a sociologist with a Ph.D., she was viewed by some as an "expert" on particular matters. However, being defined as an expert for legal purposes is different that just being someone with knowledge of particular phenomenon. On the other hand, as an agent of a defense attorney, Nicole would be seen by some as actually a private investigator, and therefore only a lay witness for purposes of testimony. There was also the question of just what it was she was supposed to be doing. Was it her purpose to argue on behalf of defendants, or to provide opinion for the court. As Nicole says, "He (the attorney) had no idea what he was asking me to do on that first case. And, of course, I had no idea either. Losing that first case was really a consequence of just not knowing what was going on, and how to approach the sentencing process. But I learned so much from losing that first case. Basically, I learned that if the mitigation was done the right way, the result was always no death penalty."

So here we now have a new kind of job title: mitigation. According to Nicole, "Mitigation is an investigation in to the *person*, not the crime. Mitigation focuses on developing an explanation as to why a crime occurred. Culpability is not at issue in mitigation. I use sociology to try to figure out why this particular person, given these sets of social variables, was led to act in a given way. In a death penalty trial mitigation is used not to determine guilt or innocence, but is used at sentencing to help determine death versus life in prison. However, appropriately used, mitigation is not something you do only after a trial has concluded and the only question is sentencing. Mitigation can, and should be used to inform the attorney about who their client is, to inform the judge so that he or she can make appropriate rulings throughout the case, and to inform the jury. In any case there may be aggravating and mitigating factors. Aggravating factors are defined by statute. For example, in the commission of a crime the criminal either had a gun or they did not have a gun. This is a matter of fact, and the presence of an aggravating factor brings into play certain legal conditions and requisites. However, mitigating factors are less rigid, and allow for the introduction of qualitative factors, such as one's upbringing, level of education, emotional state, etc. According to Nicole, "Mitigating factors are more about feeling, about how any of us process information in a given circumstance. What did the situation mean to the defendant? One thing I have found out, having worked with killers is that most of the time, despite circumstances, people kill because they perceive that they are somehow defending themselves. I've seen grown men who've felt a need to defend themselves from children." While cases such as the latter are nearly always significant distortions of reality, it is important to understand the role of their perceptions. "Ultimately," according to Nicole, "the function of mitigation is to provide a cultural translation of the case, relative to the legal proceedings, so that all parties concerned have an appropriate understanding of what has happened. Most of the time this means that the actual legal charges are reduced. In my most recent case the state had initially pursued a first degree murder charge, with the possibility of the death penalty, against one young man. After the findings of the mitigation were presented, the case was settled to manslaughter one, due to extreme emotional duress."

Presently a number of states have begun self studies related to discriminatory practices among various law enforcement agencies. In some states this has taken the form of statistical analyses of routine traffic stops on interstate highways. And some states have been turning up data which may support the claims of civil rights groups that law enforcement is uneven at best, and significantly discriminatory at worst. Questions have also risen regarding the employment of the death penalty. According to Nicole, "Low income people, people of color, and people with low levels of education, often simply cannot explain well enough just what happened. As a result, the interpretatiobyof the authorities, and the rest of the local community, is that some hideous, cold-blooded crime took place. In actuality, while a bad thing did happen, it may be something else from a legal standpoint. This is really just a problem of understanding the crime. My testimony often consists of a kind of sociology 101, in which I begin to introduce basic social behavioral concepts, and then move on to issues such as the family violence literature, and the fact that an individual often has a lot less to say about their own behavior than is often believed."

Since beginning her work in mitigation, Nicole has not returned to teaching in any significant way. She says, "I have really found it fascinating work." So, beginning in 1989, Nicole set up a private practice related to mitigation of death penalty cases. The work that she did would be considered contract work. However, as was noted earlier, Nicole was breaking new ground, so there was no real blueprint as to how to get into this kind of work, let alone set up a business to facilitate it. Essentially Nicole was doing social histories, guided by social bonding theory, in which she investigated and described the attachment, commitment and belief bonds of acused individuals before they went to court. "I was getting paid $30 an hour, which was pretty good money then. But by the end of that first summer, the Indigent Defense Fund, from which I was being paid, was now indebted to me for a substantial amount of money. In fact, they were out of money. Now, at that time I was a single mother of two, with no other job because I thought I was going to be paid for the work I'd done." The upshot of all this was that Nicole declared bankruptcy and took another position as a social worker. In a way, back where she had started. But, she continued to do death penalty work part time.

Eventually the case load for death penalty investigations became so great that Nicole was actually turning down attorneys' requests. Since she was still a full time social worker her time available for mitigation was limited. But after three years, with her bankruptcy finally cleared, and with the state having fixed the Indigent Defense Fund (she was getting checks now for work done), Nicole quite her social work job and went into private practice full time. This is where Nicole found herself, again, in the definitional vacuum of job title. Was she a sociologist with a Ph.D., and therefore some kind of expert witness, or was she a private investigator, and therefore a lay witness. In any case, she was still accomplishing the task of mitigation on behalf of defendants in death penalty cases. "The first thing I did was to determine if I needed a license for what I was doing. So, I went to the state Board of Health, which licensed psychologists, counselors, etc., and presented to them what it was that I'd been doing: that I researched cases and presented the information found to attorneys, and sometimes judges and juries if I testify. The Board of Health said 'no,' I was not going to be 'treating' anyone. Next I went to this private investigation commission and asked them if they wanted to license me? Somehow or another I'd stepped into some kind of strange political situation, and that commission said that they did not want to license my 'research'." In part because of this, Nicole went to work for the federally funded Capital Case Resources, as a mitigation specialist. But that funding lasted just a short time, and Nicole found herself back in private practice again, and still without a license to certify her work.

While with Capital Case Resources Nicole had had a court ruling that as an employee of a lawyer, doing work for that lawyer in a case, she did not need a license to do the kind of research she was doing, or to present that research in court. So, when she returned to private practice she simply acquired a business license in order to start up. She also had already developed a clientele, and was connected to the local legal scene. Added to this is the fact that there are not too many people who do mitigation. So, Nicole had work. It was just a matter of how she would proceed.

To date, Nicole has worked over 70 death penalty case mitigations. As mentioned earlier, she lost her first case, and she lost her second one as well. Both defendants were sentenced to death. Since then, however, Nicole has not lost another case. All of her cases since those first two have been resolved short of the death penalty. According to Nicole, "The reason I am successful is my sociology background. In addition, I am now doing much of my work at trial level where we can negotiate a plea bargain. Post conviction is a whole new ballgame. But the sociological insights

I have work well in this kind of legal system. I work for defense attorneys, but I'm also working for a larger community when I do mitigation. While the state does not have positions for me, I do see the day coming when they will. Further, I see the state coming to value social science graduates more and more as time goes on. This is facilitated by the general move, across the nation, to mediation rather than trial." However, there was at least one more major bump in the road for Nicole. The private investigation commission, which had earlier shown no interest in licensing Nicole's work, now served Nicole with a cease and desist order, claiming that she was doing private investigation without a license. This was a rather bizarre situation, to say the least. As things developed, Nicole concluded that the commission was creating a statutory violation as a means of broadening their own authority. In short, this was a way of regulating a developing profession, which was potentially quite lucrative.

Today Nicole's business is thriving. She has a track record of success, and she has broad-based experience across the social service and sociological spectrum. For death penalty cases Nicole earns about $85 per hour, and "There are many, many, many hours of research in any death penalty case," according to Nicole. Her annual income is in the range of $80,000 per year. While Nicole is a Ph.D., and is therefore deemed an expert for witness purposes, she sees evidence of the field continuing to develop, and along with it opportunities for those at the bachelors level. With a BA/BS, according to Nicole, new professionals expect to earn from $45,000 to $60,000 per year, depending on various circumstances. Among other things, Nicole advises students to really sharpen their writing skills. Without these then there is no way to adequately present your insights. But, you must have insights to offer. For this reason Nicole is a very strong advocate of the social sciences, sociology in particular, as preparation for this kind of work. "Anyone can ask questions, " says Nicole, "but you have to know why you are asking the questions you are asking. If you do, then you are in position to do quite well in the field."

When asked, "So what is your job title now?", Nicole answers, "I am a sociologist who specializes in mitigation. Not only do I do mitigation research, but I also do mediation, and have a certification in the field. Finally, I did eventually get my private investigator license, in the midst of all these 'wranglings' with the state commission. And, this is the license with which I practice. But, I am still a sociologist." In conclusion, Nicole says, "This has been wonderful work. I love this work, and I recommend it to others."

24

JUVENILE JUSTICE

Helen Ramsey has a story to tell, and she will tell anyone who will listen. It is an inspiring story, one full of tragedy, but also always as full of hope and victory. It is a story which continues to unfold. Since 1974, Helen has been a Youth Center Administrator for a pre-trial juvenile detention center in the northeast. Since January of 1998, Helen has also been a state Assemblywoman. This is a long way from what Helen calls her "crabgrass and diaper-rash years" as a mom, wife, and homemaker. It is an even longer way from days when, as a child caught in the capricious winds of war, she spent three years in a Japanese concentration camp. Yet somehow each experience in her life prepared her for the work she has been doing in juvenile justice for the past 25 years. One source characterizes Helen and her work in the following way: "Helen rubs shoulders everyday with boys from urban killer gangs, groups named the Lynch Mob, the Sons of Malcolm X, the Eight Ball Posse. When 15 year old Jason started calling her, 'my main lady,' she knew she was in. Word on the streets say, Helen 'walks the talk'." Not bad for a woman of 66.

In 1953, Helen graduated from a small Christian liberal arts college in the Midwest with majors in speech, psychology, and education. According to Helen, "In 1953 women graduating from college could be teachers, secretaries, or nurses. Or at least it certainly seemed like that." After a couple of years teaching in the Midwest Helen and her husband moved, eventually ending up in the northeast. Shortly thereafter Helen went to work in an inner-city high school for 5 ½ years, teaching English, journalism, sponsoring the school newspaper and choir, and generally being involved in all aspects of her student's lives. In her second year the students voted to dedicate the school yearbook to her. As she recalls, "I found out that one young man from my home room class had gone around the school threatening, or otherwise 'persuading' students to vote for me!"

What was it that made this young man do such a thing? In fact, what made all the students Helen touched try so hard, accomplish so much, and support her so thoroughly? Well, there were a variety of things which might provide some insight. She was active and aggressive. She was more like them than the other 70 "blue-hairs" teaching there. She was firm. She cared about them. She went beyond the norm of teacher-student relationships. She challenged them beyond their own expectations. She held out hope for them. She listened to them. Obviously, these seem now like the right ingredients in a recipe for success. But there was something else going on. When we try to evaluate such relationships we often get only half the picture. We see what Helen did to those students to create such startling results. But the other half of the relationship is what the students were doing. They were, at least initially, watching, listening, observing, evaluating, defining, and otherwise taking stock of Helen. Now, 40 years later Helen can see what was happening. In her words, "You never know who is watching you. I've come to learn that in a new encounter you have nine seconds to make a first impression. So, it matters what you are saying and doing. Without knowing it you are repeatedly making first impressions. And what those impressions are, matters. I like to call it, 'footprints that last forever'." One of those "footprints" made a lasting imprint on that young man who muscled his schoolmates into that yearbook dedication vote. He caught her message of challenge and hope, and made his way first to the university and then on to law school. But how can we be sure it was Helen's footprints?

It had been about 10 to 12 years since Helen had quite teaching in order to have and raise children. She called these her "crabgrass and diaper-rash years." She was taking care of the household, raising her kids, teaching Sunday School. While this was good for her, she also had notions of somehow being more involved. She joined the League of Women Voters and tried to be current on community issues. Among other things the League kept an eye on the politicians, both present and future. One day she saw the name of that same young man from her home room. He seemed to be an "up-and comer" in local politics, and she interviewed him for the League. Then a major surprise occurred. He came to Helen's house and told her he was planning on running for political office. In most places we would call the office a county commissioner. The problem was that local politics had always had the ring of the "machine." If not part of the machine, then election was not likely. But the kid from the home room nonetheless asked Helen to run his campaign. According to Helen, "I had no experience in politics, let alone running a campaign, and we were up against machine politics." Somehow, they won!

Now elected, the new commissioner was given responsibility for the county's juvenile detention center. It was a sore spot in the county, and being the new commissioner he had to take what he was given. In 1973, a 14 year old boy hung himself at the detention center. In 1974, a writer for a major newspaper did an investigative report on the center calling it unfit for animals and urging the state to take action. Subsequent to this all kinds of other investigations, including the commissioner's, concluded that things were awful and something had to be done. In the meantime Helen had taken a position as the commissioner's administrative assistant. She had an up-close picture of all that was going on with the center. It was apparent that the old ways of doing things, including the old administrator of the center, had to go. But what to do? According to Helen, "After seeing all that was wrong with the center, and seeing also that solutions seemed in short supply, I went to the commissioner and said, 'why not me?' It was a completely new field for me, and I had no experience in it. But, he had complete trust in me, and he knew what I was made of. Besides, we had already won an election, even though we had had no experience with that either."

Helen's position was that of Administrator. She did not come up through any ranks of the profession. While she demonstrated an amazing ability to know all the boys under her care, up to 1,500 per year, her real job was to somehow redirect the organization. She had to change entrenched attitudes, both within the institution and throughout the surrounding community. Because this was her real job the

110

remainder of this CP will focus on the skills and perspectives which Helen demonstrated, and believes are necessary to success in her line of work.

Soon after being appointed Helen was called out of a party at her hone to quell a riot at the center. "The problem was that literally everyone at the center, staff and kids alike had a grievance. The previous administration was 'old school.' It was male dominated and oriented to authority and control." Predictably, the various groupings of people at the center, kids and staff alike, had developed patterns of mutual mis-trust and antagonism. Helen's initial response was to listen. She went to the cells where the kids had been routinely locked down, handcuffed to steel beds bolted to the floor, and sprayed with mace. She asked them, one by one, to tell her their stories. She also listened to the staff. According to Helen, "They knew they were just barely hanging on to things at the center, and it certainly was not a productive work environment. Many were afraid. None were trained. "But I was inexperienced. I had to somehow learn, and learn quickly. So, I initiated an open door policy. I wanted them to tell me what was going on. And, when they wouldn't come to me, I went to them. I walked the grounds, sat in cells, at tables, and in offices. I brought in the commissioner too. He sat with staff, employees of the county, his employees, and he also listened."

Listening was one thing. It was the start of a different kind of relationship. Helen now needed to follow through. But she had no real resources. If those were to come at all they would be coming later. For now it was important to see some change, any change, tangible or symbolic. Part of the problem was the way in which all people at the center saw themselves, and each other. For example, the staff saw inmates. Helen decided that this needed to be changed. Children would no longer be called inmates, they would be students or residents. Likewise, guards would now be officers. Her logic was that the name brought with it a perspective. If you see an "inmate" you will act as if you are around an inmate. But if you see a "student," your whole perspective changes. Helen also got rid of the uniforms. Uniforms, in her perspective, maintained the old order and old way of doing things. Letting them wear something of their own reminded everyone that these were children, not inmates. It seemed to make a difference.

Next came the outside resources. The needs were enormous. Helen found that the teacher at the center had a budget which provided 50 cents per child per year! Just fifty cents! Helen knew that as much as she would work within the center, she had to make the case to the community at large. "I had to get out and tell our story." Helen did this in a variety of ways. She wrote articles and press releases noting changes at the center and celebrating its victories. She went wherever she could get an audience and told them what was happening. She always had a story. She made the children seem like children, not inmates, because they had names and lives and dreams. She went to the politicians, demanding the resources necessary to do the job. "If you don't ask you won't get," is a common phrase among those who have learned how to raise such support. She joined professional associations and networked to the resources they had. She became the first woman president of the state's Juvenile Detention Association. In short order a number of significant results were being produced. Grants began rolling in, for everything from paper, glue and construction paper, to officer training, to federally funded construction of a new building and, a new name; County Youth Center versus Children's Shelter. It was a complete makeover of facilities, relationships, perceptions, and definitions. But the work is still ongoing, and not every new dream is fulfilled. Tragedy still occurs,

111

though the battle has been fully engaged.

Whatever else the present day County Youth Center is, it is most defiantly a movement. Yes, it has a place and a structure to its organization, but it is always evolving. Because of this, according to Helen, the perspectives and skills she has employed to help remake it are as valid and necessary today as ever they were. Such perspectives and skills constitute Helen's advice to student's today who believe they are called to make a difference in the lives of children. "The number one skill to develop," according to Helen, "is communication. If you can't communicate then you cannot do this job. Furthermore, you must be able to communicate with all kinds of people and in all kinds of contexts. You have to be able to counsel one-on-one. You must be able to write a cogent letter, report, or grant. You must feel at ease in the presence of political and economic power holders, and be able to articulate your mission to them. You need to have empathy for families. And you need the guts to speak in front of hundreds or even thousands. But, this is just half the skill of communication. You must learn to become an active listener. You need to know when it is time to speak, and when it is time to just shut up and listen."

Networking is another necessary tool. According to Helen, "It does matter who you know, and how you are known. You must make it a point to meet people under any circumstance. Even if you have no idea how you may come together in the future. This is my point about 'footprints that last forever.' You just never know who is watching, and how you are impacting others. Therefore, everyone can be critical to your future in some way."

Helen's future now includes the title of state Assemblywoman. According to Helen, "I was not seeking political office. However, an incumbent Assemblyman came and asked me to be his running-mate. As we talked about the possibilities he asked for my resume. I actually have two. One is a traditional resume which is essentially a list of my past. But I also have another, non-traditional resume. In it I write out my dreams and accomplishments. It is more of a story of who I am. When I gave these to the Assemblymen I really got his attention. So I recommended both kinds of resumes. And have them ready now. You never know when your future will come knocking."

Today Helen is busy balancing the duties of both youth center administration and Assemblywoman. Her life is hectic, she is always on the go. Her work and high profile now make her an in-demand speaker, conference and workshop consultant all across the country. Helen has received numerous recognitions for such work. Among them Helen has received the highest awards from the National Juvenile Detention Association and the state chapter of the American Correctional Association. She now passes on her expertise as a trainer/consultant for the National Academy of Corrections and through contributions to major journals and newspapers such as the New York Times, Philadelphia Inquirer, and Fort Worth Telegram. She has also finally begun to achieve some level of financial reward. She earns approximately $70,000 per year as an administrator; up from the less than $10,000 per year she earned her first year. She also earns an additional $35,000 per year as an Assemblywoman. However, in this kind of work Helen's real rewards are measured in changed lives, not dollars and cents. Helen speaks of these as gifts. What she does is to pass along the gifts of others to her kids at the center. The dream is that they will someday pass it on to another.

112

25

WHERE DO WE GO FROM HERE?

Step 3: From Exploration and Assumption to Choice and Challenge

Exploration
Having reached this chapter I might be inclined to assume that you have read all that precedes it. However, that would be contrary to my own advice regarding assumptions in the design of this book. On the other hand there is a logic to contemplating next steps at this point. In general, I hope that your explorations in criminal justice have resulted first of all in an enhanced understanding of the breadth of the field. Secondly, I hope that your assumptions have begun to be replaced, via the CP's, by information and experience. But it is the next steps which are most critical; choice and challenge.

The issue of breadth was clearly evident not only by the range of CP's presented, but by the variety of skills and roles any one criminal justice professional would likely employ. So, we were introduced to professionals in forensic anthropology, political office, civilians and sworn officers, federal, state and local departments, prosecutors, police chiefs and sheriffs, wardens, men and women. We met professionals with degrees in law, business, social work, anthropology, geography, law enforcement, sociology, psychology and education. We also met professionals with no degrees beyond high school. These same professionals suggested that students should make sure that they have an understanding of history, cultures, languages, computers, accounting, communications, chemistry, interpersonal relations, family studies, etc., etc., etc. Such professionals are expected to conduct themselves with integrity, empathy, honesty, common sense, discernment, courage, skill in finances and be in good physical condition. They must know the law and be willing to train and learn without ceasing. They have to be able to deal with career criminals of the worst sort, a public that is often is fearful or at least distant, yet be leaders in disasters, speak in schools to our children, find lost pets and break bad news to families.

Do you feel somewhat overwhelmed? Do you wonder if you are up to the task? If not maybe you should be. You must be realistic about this field. In being realistic it is just as important to know your limits as well as your interests. One task of college is to find out what interests you. Another equally important task is to find out what doesn't.

Assumptions

The second objective is to develop a perspective based on information and experience, not assumptions. As we investigate the CP's we see that careers are virtually always in motion. Things change. They change in a variety of ways which we might be able to categorize. Perhaps the most persistent source is the environment or the work context. Communities grow and develop, interstate highways bring traffic to rural or remote areas, computers increase our pace of life, events around the world ripple towards us, and our families grow and mature. In the introduction, I suggested that personal change is also fundamental. Remember the following question? "Are you now the person you want to be in the next 10 to 20 years?" I have yet to find a student to answer yes to this question. To say you want to be different in some ways is not an indictment of who you are now, but is a recognition that we all must develop as we engage our world. In each of the CP's we see how personal and circumstantial change has been an integral part of each respective career. But is this inevitability of change simply something out of our hands?

The answer to the above question is yes and no. Many, perhaps even most of the agents of change lie outside your immediate control or sphere of influence. Some things, such as natural disasters just happen. Occasionally societal development seems just as spontaneous; for example the fall of the Soviet empire or apartheid South Africa. Even personal change can seem to surprise us. We wake up one day and are suddenly dissatisfied with our station in life, or a friend or family member suddenly traipses off to a new life. However, there is a solution to the seeming capriciousness of change. That is, anticipate it, expect it, look for it. This does not mean that you can never rest easy, but it does mean that you understand that change on a variety of fronts is inevitable. By being proactive regarding change your opportunity for influencing its direction and scope is significantly enhanced.

Choice

What this brings us to is the role of choice. None of the CP's evidenced fate. Some have certainly had good fortune, or have been in the right place at the right time. However, all have had to exercise choice about their careers. Recall that the CP subjects have a lot of advice for you. For example, take courses such as communications, and computer science, search out internships, learn habits of conduct which include respect, politeness, and integrity, learn a second language, and be a keen observer of people. Some of these offers of advice may actually be of specific interest to you, but some others may not be so attractive. For example, while you perhaps are eager to just finish an undergraduate degree, are you prepared for the continuous training/education required to keep the career you know covet? Remember the 780 hours of specialized training completed by Larry (crime scene analyst)? Regardless of you answer, understand that what you do requires an effective choice, one which leads to action. The CP's are recommending that you make such choices. But what about the flip side? What if you do not make the choice? What then? Be certain of this. Failing to choose is not the same as a choice not made. Be assured of this. When you don't choose, someone else will.

Challenge

OK, you recognize the breadth of criminal justice, the pervasiveness of change, and your responsibility for choice. So, as the chapter title asks, "Where do we go from here?" My suggestion is to go beyond the information and experience of this book and begin to see for yourself. One way of doing this is to use the CP's as models for your own research. By this I mean, investigate the careers of those who have gone before you. Check with your faculty or department for names of alumni who are now in the field. Contact them and get their story. Or, ask that such people be brought back to school to meet with students. If this is not possible there are always local practitioners in criminal justice. As with this book, I found them most willing and eager to share their stories. Ask, there is little to lose and much to gain. But of course, this requires a choice.

Now I realize that such opportunities are not evenly distributed. Some of you are part of active and aggressive departments and such a personal challenge is easy. For others the challenge is more daunting. For all who are interested there is yet another source which is even now developing new structures of opportunity, the Internet. Simply type in "Careers in Criminal Justice" and you have tapped into the tip of the iceberg of information available to you. Check out specific agency or department Web pages, such as the Federal Bureau of Prisons, the FBI, various state police (i.e., Illinois State Police), and even local and metropolitan police departments (i.e., Los Angeles Police Department). Just type them in by name and explore the vast array of connections within the profession.

So, now we have come full circle. At the beginning you were exploring via some course, and this small book. It is not a bad start, regardless of your present career ambitions. But it is also just a start. Now it is time to make some choices and take hold of the challenge. It is your career, and I look forward to what you make of it.

NOTES

NOTES

NOTES

NOTES

NOTES